DIVING
HAWAII

DIVING
HAWAII

By Steve Rosenberg

AQUA QUEST PUBLICATIONS, INC. — NEW YORK

PUBLISHER'S NOTE

The Aqua Quest *Diving* series offers extensive information on dive sites as well as topside activities.

At the time of publication, the information contained in this book was determined to be as accurate and up-to-date as possible. The reader should bear in mind, however, that dive site terrain and landmarks can change due to weather or construction. In addition, new dive shops, restaurants, hotels and shops can open and existing ones close. Telephone numbers are subject to change as are government regulations.

The publisher welcomes the reader's comments and assistance to help ensure the accuracy of future editions of this book.

Good diving and enjoy your stay!

Library of Congress Catalog Card Number: 90-82635
ISBN 0-9623389-1-5

All photographs are by the author.
Design By Richard Liu

Printed in Hong Kong
10 9 8 7 6 5 4 3 2

ACKNOWLEDGEMENTS

Thank you to my understanding wife, Kathleen and to the many who contributed their time and efforts: Dick Dresie, Nik Konstantinou of Sea Sage Diving Center, Pete Ricciardi of Aquatics Kauai, Lisa Choquette of Dive Makai Charters, Ed Robinson of Hawaiian Watercolors, Blain Roberts of Lahaina Divers, Central Pacific Divers, Gene Clark of Leeward Dive Center, Jackie James of Aloha Dive Shop, Brad Revis and Jim Beat of Ocean Adventures. And, a special thanks to my good friends Jim and Julie Robinson of Kona Coast Divers for their assistance, input and encouragement in putting this book together.

CONTENTS

FOREWORD

A year-round pleasant climate, spectacular scenery and beaches, warm Pacific waters, friendly people and a beautiful underwater environment have made Hawaii one of the world's most popular vacation spots.

Diving in Hawaii is excellent and is especially noted for its unusual underwater terrain and its diversity of beautiful marine life — about 30 percent of which is unique to the Islands. The frogfish, harlequin shrimp, Hawaiian turkeyfish and the Spanish dancer nudibranch are only a few of the remarkable animals found in Hawaiian waters. The underwater habitat runs the gamut from coral reefs and drop-offs to the stark beauty of lava formed tunnels, caves, caverns, fissures, pinnacles and tubes.

Forty-seven of the best dive sites in the Islands — both shore and boat dives — are covered in detail in this guide while an additional 21 sites are described briefly in an appendix. Also included is a chapter on marine life — both the rare indigenous species and the potentially hazardous.

While this guide was written specifically for the diver, it also provides extensive information on topside activities that both the diver and non-diver will enjoy. There is a separate chapter on each of the four major islands: Oahu, Maui, Hawaii and Kauai. For each of these islands, a brief introduction is given as well as information on how to get there and the best places for divers to stay. A section on "exploring" suggests various driving routes on each island and identifies major points of interest. Three other islands, Niihau, Lanai and Molokai, are covered in brief as dive site locations.

Hawaii is a unique destination for a diving vacation. It offers beauty and excitement underwater, and a topside tropical paradise that the whole family will enjoy.

Steve Rosenberg
Union City, California
June 1990

CHAPTER I THE HAWAIIAN ISLANDS

THE PAST

The Polynesians, traveling in double-hulled sailing canoes across 2,000 miles of open ocean, are believed to be the first people to settle in the Hawaiian Islands. Isolated from other cultures for about a thousand years, they instituted a caste system ruled by chiefs.

In 1778, Captain James Cook discovered the Hawaiian Islands while heading from Tahiti to America's West Coast to search for a northwest passage, a supposed seaway link beween the Pacific and Atlantic Oceans. He first landed upon Kauai where the Hawaiians thought he was one of their gods. On a return visit to Kealakekua Bay on the Island of Hawaii, Cook was killed when a fight broke out between the Hawaiians and his crew.

Within a span of 17 years after Cook's death, King Kamehameha I, using western arms and advisers, conquered Maui and Oahu and united all of Hawaii under his rule. It was Kamehameha I who gave the Westerners their foothold in the Islands.

The first sugar plantation was started on the island of Kauai in 1835. In 1850, the Masters and Servants Act was passed, establishing an immigration board to import plantation workers. Between 1850 and 1930, almost 400,000 Japanese; Filipinos, Chinese and Portuguese immigrated to the Islands, becoming the base for Hawaii's diverse ethnic community.

At the turn of the century, Hawaii became a territory of the United States. In the early 20th century, the Hawaiian economy as well as its politics were controlled by the "Big Five," a complex of firms which owned most of the sugar trade. Socioeconomic changes, including development of the International Labor Workers Union, began to undermine their power. In 1959, Hawaii became the 50th state, and tourism increased quickly, becoming the major industry of the Islands.

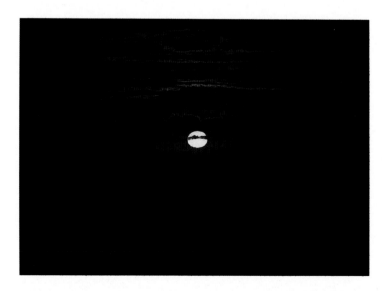

The Big Island of Hawaii is the orchid capital of the world. Countless varieties of this flower are grown in the Hilo area.

Hawaii's gorgeous sunsets are among the most beautiful to be found anywhere and create a romantic setting for a walk on the beach or add a special treat to a boat dive.

THE PRESENT

The Hawaiian Islands form an archipelago which stretches more than 1,000 miles across the central Pacific Ocean. The actual land area, however, is quite small, totaling 6,471 square miles. There are eight major islands, all of which are clustered at the southeastern end of the archipelago. Of these, Kahoolawe is a bombing range for the U.S. Navy and Niihau is privately owned, leaving Oahu, Maui, Kauai, Hawaii (the Big Island), Lanai and Molokai as potential vacation destinations. Coral reefs, sandy beaches and impressive lava formations surround each of the individual islands.

The islands of Hawaii are all of volcanic origin. Openings in the earth's crust spewed forth molten rock which eventually broke the surface of the Pacific, creating the islands. Although the volcanoes that created the older islands are extinct, Kilauea and Mauna Loa are still active and continue to add to the size of the Big Island (Hawaii).

The highest peak is Mauna Kea, on the island of Hawaii which rises 13,796 feet above sea level and extends almost 20,000 feet to the ocean floor. Because of their origin, all the islands have mountainous terrain.

It is due to these mountains that rainfall can vary from less than ten inches a year to more than 400 inches on different sides of the same island. The climate, volcanic soil and isolation in the central Pacific Ocean have resulted in the development of endemic flora and fauna. The introduction of plants and animals from other parts of the world has augmented this variety. Today, Hawaii is one of only a few states where sugarcane is grown, and the only state where coffee, macadamia nuts and pineapples are grown commercially.

Tourism, however, is Hawaii's number one industry. The unbeatable combination of a year-round pleasant climate, beautiful scenery and beaches, friendly people, and a spectacular underwater environment make Hawaii the perfect vacation spot for divers and non-divers alike.

USEFUL INFORMATION

Getting to the Islands. Honolulu International Airport, on the island of Oahu, has become one of the busiest airports in the United States. All travelers from overseas must enter the Islands via Honolulu. Domestic travelers have the option of flying to Honolulu or directly to one of the other islands. A variety of American carriers, including United, Hawaiian, Continental, American, Trans World Air, Delta, Northwest and Pan American, fly regular schedules to Honolulu. Several airlines fly directly to the Big Island, Maui and Kauai.

Non-stop flights from the mainland are now available from a number of cities in the East, Midwest and Southwest. Flights from the Pacific Coast originate primarily from San Francisco and Los Angeles, but at times are also available from San Diego, Oakland, Seattle and Anchorage. Flying time from the West Coast averages 4 1/2 to 5 hours.

A number of international carriers regularly service Honolulu including Japan Airlines, All Nippon Airways, Philippine Airlines, China Airlines, Singapore Airlines, C.P. Air and Qantas. All foreign travelers must obtain valid passports and entry visas.

Where to Stay. Hawaii offers a wide variety of accommodations including five star hotels, bed and breakfast inns, condominiums with or without kitchens, private homes, youth hostels and campgrounds.

A good travel agent can help in making the right selection. One hassle-free way of planning a trip is to book a package tour. Island Holidays, Maupintour, Cartan, Tauck, Roberts, Pleasant Hawaiian Holidays, Classic Hawaii, Sun Tours and American Express are among the large companies offering tours with a range of options and prices. In addition to lodging, many packages include air travel, meals and ground transportation.

Snorkeling and diving can be an exciting, romantic activity for vacationing couples to share and enjoy.

Waikiki has become the symbol of the Hawaiian vacation and hosts a large percentage of the tourists who visit the Islands.

Bed and breakfast inns are becoming popular in Hawaii. On Maui, the Plantation Inn is an excellent one that is specifically designed for divers. For families and dive groups, a good way to cut expenses is to rent condominiums with kitchens.

For tips on dining, shopping and entertainment, as well as an update on weekly events, pick up a copy of *This Week*, *Spotlight Hawaii* and *Guide* magazines, which are available free at the airports on each island. These publications are updated weekly and offer valuable discount coupons.

Inter-Island Travel. The islands are only a short flight apart making it convenient to include two or more islands in a single visit. Wikiwiki buses provide free shuttle service between the international and inter-island terminals of the Honolulu Airport. Several airlines make regularly scheduled flights between the islands. Aloha Airlines and Hawaiian Airlines, Hawaii's major carriers, provide the most frequent inter-island jet service. There are also a number of airlines which use smaller passenger planes including Reeves, Princeville Airways and Air Molokai.

Climate. Hawaii's climate is characterized by mild temperatures, moderate humidity and prevailing northeasterly trade winds throughout most of the year. Two remarkable features of the climate are the drastic differences in rainfall within very short distances and the very few severe storms.

Generally, there are only two seasons in Hawaii: summer and winter. During the summer season (May through September), the weather is warmer and dryer, and the trade winds are more persistent. During the winter season (October through April), the weather is cooler, and the trade winds are often overcome by other weather patterns. The average temperature fluctuates from 71 degrees in the winter to 78 in the summer. November through March are usually the wettest months.

Hawaii's mountains have a significant impact on weather and climate. Because of the diversity of terrain among the individual islands, there is a tremendous variety of micro-climates not only from island to island, but also between different areas of the same island. Over the open sea near Hawaii, rainfall averages between 25 and 30 inches a year. However, in areas where warm, moist winds are forced to rise over the windward coasts, the rainfall can exceed 400 inches per year. In the areas sheltered by terrain, rainfall can be less than 15 inches per year.

The hibiscus is one of the many beautiful flowers that thrive in Hawaii's tropical climate.

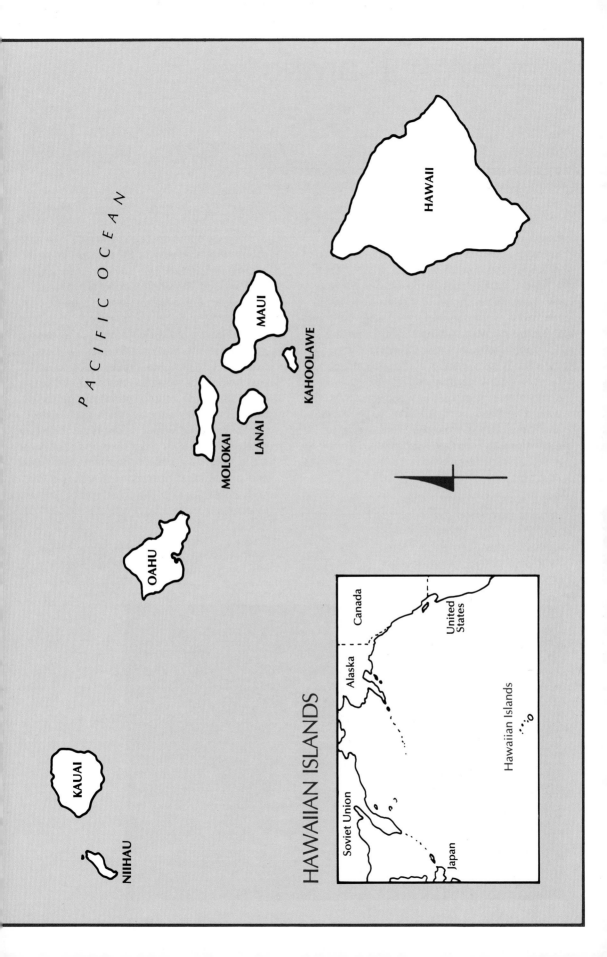

HAWAIIAN ISLANDS

PACIFIC OCEAN

KAUAI

NIIHAU

OAHU

MOLOKAI

LANAI

MAUI

KAHOOLAWE

HAWAII

Soviet Union

Japan

Alaska

Canada

United States

Hawaiian Islands

CHAPTER II DIVING

Scuba diving in Hawaii is noted for its unusual underwater terrain and its diversity of beautiful and unique marine animals.

Most diving occurs in the calmer water of the leeward coastlines of the major islands. However, when the trade winds are light and there are no approaching storms or strong Kona winds, the daily heating and cooling of the islands gives rise to light, onshore sea breezes during the day and warm, offshore land breezes at night. During these times, the water can be calm on all sides of the islands and divers can explore the often inaccessible reefs along the northern and eastern coasts.

Soft octocoral appears to be a smooth, hard coral but is actually soft to the touch. This animal is characterized by individual polyps that have eight feathery tentacles.

Water temperatures range from 72 degrees in the winter season to 80 degrees in the summer season. At least a full length eighth inch wetsuit is recommended not only for warmth, but also for protection against cuts, scrapes and stinging creatures.

Visibility varies widely from island to island and site to site, but on calm days it often exceeds 100 feet. Most dive shops have an excellent stock of rental gear, so you can leave the heavy, cumbersome equipment at home and bring only as much as you want to pack. For non-divers, Hawaii is an excellent place to snorkel or even take an introductory scuba dive with one of the many experienced and professional operations. If you get the "bug," Hawaii is a wonderful place to learn to dive!

Drop-offs offer impressive underwater landscapes. This one is dotted with cauliflower coral.

UNDERWATER HABITATS

There are five main types of underwater habitats in the Islands: coral reefs, tubes, caves and caverns formed by lava, drop-offs, basalt boulders and sandy bottoms.

Coral reefs. The most conspicuous, diverse and colorful of the shallow-water communities are those of the corals which form both fringing and sub-tidal reefs. The islands of Kauai, Oahu, Maui, Molokai and Lanai are partially ringed by coral reefs, a combination of limestone secreting corals, coraline algae and other plants and animals.

Wave action, water temperature and available light are important in determining which corals are able to grow in given areas. Cauliflower and lobe corals are sturdy corals which dominate the reefs where there is considerable wave action and good available light. More fragile forms of coral, such as finger corals, are found mostly on deeper reefs or in shallow protected bays.

The active growing part of the reef is the seaward edge, where most corals are found. Sea urchins, especially the slate-pencil urchins and the long-spined urchins, will be found in this area. Among fishes frequenting the seaward edge of the reefs are brilliantly-hued butterflyfishes, parrotfishes, wrasses and

surgeonfishes, which feed on coral polyps, algae and plankton. On the reef flat, damselfishes and wrasses predominate. Octopuses, spiny lobsters and squirrelfishes will be found hiding in the many crevices and caves throughout the reef.

There is no fringing reef on the island of Hawaii. The Kona and Kohala Coasts instead have extensively developed sub-tidal reefs which are never exposed above water. Sub-tidal reefs exhibit an even greater diversity of animal life than do the fringing reefs. These are the areas where spectacular shells including tiger cowries, triton trumpets, and various miter and cone shells will be found. Butterflyfishes, tangs, trumpetfish and forcepsfish abound, attracted by the foods and diverse habitats available within the sub-tidal coral reefs.

In many shoreline areas of Kauai, Oahu and Maui, there are calcareous benches in the intertidal zone. This area is alternately covered and exposed by the sea during tidal changes and the flat surfaces of the benches are covered with a thick mat of algae. At high tide, surgeonfishes, parrotfishes and wrasses feed on this algae and the invertebrates found in these areas.

At night, moray eels will often be seen out foraging. This zebra eel, which feeds mostly on crustaceans, hunts for prey along a flat, sandy bottom.

Hawaiian waters offer both divers and snorkelers many opportunities to swim with turtles.

Lava Formations. There is a stark beauty to Hawaii's underwater terrain which is dominated by lava rock, covered in some places by a thin veneer of coral. When the outpourings of lava from active volcanoes flowed into the sea, they also carried pockets of trapped steam. As the lava cooled, the steam dissipated, leaving a rough and broken underwater reefscape honeycombed with a maze of tunnels, caves, caverns and fissures.

These areas especially offer unique habitats to a variety of marine life. Often, nocturnal animals such as squirrelfishes, bigeyes, lobster and cowries can be found in this dark, protected habitat during the day.

A fascinating aspect of diving in Hawaii are the lava tubes which developed as streams of molten lava formed crusts when cooled by the seawater. The lava gradually solidified until a stream only a few yards wide continued to flow inside the tube. At the end of an eruption, most of the molten lava flowed out the end of the tube leaving a hollow space in the middle. In the majority of lava tubes the remaining hollow space is less than 3 feet across, but a few are as wide as 45 feet.

Another legacy of the lava flows are the many pinnacles, tables and vertical walls.

Drop-offs. Marine life is plentiful along Hawaii's many impressive drop-offs where currents bring a continual supply of plankton. Plankton feeders, such as milletseed, pennant and pyramid butterflyfishes can be found schooling here. Pelagics, such as jacks, barracuda and rays will often be sighted cruising in blue water just off the walls which are themselves very colorful with varieties of corals, sponges and algae.

Basalt Boulders. In areas which are swept by heavy wave action, the underwater terrain is dominated by large, clean basalt boulders. Several species of fish, including rudderfishes, achilles tangs and surgeonfishes are often found schooling in these surgy waters.

Sand Bottoms. Between the patches of hard coral reef are usually found expanses of sand. Here, a variety of animals find shelter among the scattered coral and lava rocks or in the sand itself. Large shells and sea stars are common and the observant diver will find octopuses, scorpionfishes and lizardfishes. Schools of goatfishes and surgeonfishes can be found foraging in this area.

One of Hawaii's main dive attractions is the unusual underwater lava formations created by the flow of lava into the sea. As the lava cooled, a maze of tubes, tunnels, caves and fissures were formed.

STOP!

LAVA TUBES AND CAVES CAN BE DANGEROUS

Hawaii's lava tubes and caves are fascinating to explore. Most are safe, however even for experienced divers, penetrating enclosed, overhead environments can be dangerous.

Several of the dive sites described in this guide have extensive systems of tubes, tunnels and caves. Divers should be aware of their personal limitations and understand that such terrain can present certain dangers.

It is always wise to ask the experts at local dive centers about any potentially hazardous sites. If they recommend avoiding certain areas unless accompanied by a guide, follow their advice! Professional guides are available. Do not hesitate to ask for one to show you these unusual formations.

Whether with a guide or a dive buddy, always carry dive lights and be careful to stay off the bottom. Divers can easily become disoriented or lost in reduced visibility when fins stir up sediment that sometimes collects on the floors of tubes and caves.

Many of these sites are located in shallow water where wave action can produce strong surge. Blow holes are another danger and are often found at the end of shallow tunnels. Never dive these shallow sites when the ocean is rough.

In some areas, such as Three Room Cave on the Kona Coast, the tunnels and caverns are so extensive that dive operators will rig safety lines with blinking strobes and backup tanks.

Hawaii's lava formations offer some beautiful and exciting diving experiences which should not be missed. Safety, however, should always be the first concern.

For further information about training in cave diving contact:

The National Association for Cave Diving
P.O. Box 14492
Gainesville, FL 32604

Cave Diving Section
The National Speleological Society
P.O. Box 950
Branford, FL 32008

BOAT DIVING

Boat diving is the easiest way to experience diving in Hawaii and there are many excellent dive boat operations on all of the major islands. Each operation has its own divemasters who can take you to the best sites and, if you like, take you on an underwater guided tour.

Divemasters will always discuss each site prior to the dive as well as review the dive plan. Before entering the water, divers should know the maximum allowable depth and bottom time for each dive. It is also important that divers find out as much as possible about what there is to see, including any potential hazards that may exist.

Boats are usually tied off to moorings or anchored close to the site so that it is not necessary to swim great distances. If there is a current present, remember to swim against the current for the first part of the dive and let the current bring you back to the boat. As with all dives, always ascend very slowly and save plenty of air for a three minute safety stop at 15 feet.

SHORE DIVING

There are many interesting shore dives in the islands. However, there are a number of problems faced by visiting divers who are not familiar with the areas. As a matter of course, always consult a local dive store for locations, directions and additional information about entries, exits and potential hazards. It is not advisable to leave valuables in your car while shore diving.

A number of excellent shore dives with easy access and interesting things to see are included in this guide. The major differences between shore diving and boat diving are the entries and exits and the distance you must swim to get to your site. Of course, most popular boat dive sites are not accessible from shore. It is important to check surf conditions before each shore dive.

Each of the four major islands has excellent boat diving operations with comfortable boats and helpful crews.

Hawaii offers excellent shore diving with protected entries and exits from sandy beaches and lava shelves.

Scuba divers who come to Hawaii will find warm water with visibility often exceeding 100 feet. Most dive stores carry a wide selection of rental gear so divers need not travel with a lot of equipment.

Octopuses can often be seen
both during the day and at
night. These creatures are such
masters of disguise that they are
often difficult to spot, even
when looking directly at them.

The bright red Spanish dancer is
usually seen only at night. This
nudibranch is named after an
unusual swimming defense
mechanism it employs which
resembles a dancing motion.

NIGHT DIVING

While most diving enthusiasts are lounging around their hotel bars or on their lanais, sipping chi chi's or pina coladas and exchanging slightly exaggerated accounts of the day's adventures, there is a growing number of divers treating themselves to some of Hawaii's most fascinating and enjoyable diving.

Several hours after the sun goes down, the underwater world undergoes a remarkable transformation. A host of unusual creatures which hide or sleep during the day are active and cruising the reefs at night. In addition, many reef fishes, which are too shy to be approached in daylight, either tuck themselves into the coral to sleep at night or will cruise slowly along the bottom.

The only special equipment needed for night diving is a bright and dependable light. There are many shapes and sizes of lights available for night diving, from large, powerful lights that project bright, wide-angled beams to small lights that photographers will often mount on their strobes for illumination and aiming. It is always wise to carry a backup in case the first light fails. Most dive operations require that a chemical lightstick (cyalume) be affixed to snorkels or scuba tanks so that divers will be easy to spot on the surface should their lights fail.

Night dives are the time to see Hawaii's colorful reef fishes up close and afford a great opportunity for photographers to get pictures of parrotfishes, butterflyfishes, surgeonfishes and others that are impossible to approach during the day.

There are a variety of marine animals that hide deep in holes and cracks during the day, venturing forth to feed at night. Among these are many interesting invertebrates, with odd shapes and fascinating behaviors. Spiny urchins and pencil urchins, which are normally wedged into cracks and crevices during the day, move into the open at night on short, specialized spines. Cowry shells, cloaked in their camouflaged mantles, suddenly appear, along with varieties of shrimp with flamboyant colors, such as the tiny harlequin. Lobsters, including the distinct hairy Hawaiian lobster, climb stiff-legged from their holes to join the other nocturnal predators.

This is also the time when octopuses prowl the reef and moray eels are often encountered winding their way over the bottom, foraging for food. Large conger eels can also be seen searching for sleeping fish.

If you have never made a night dive before, Hawaii is a wonderful place to start!

Most night diving is highlighted by a variety of fascinating marine animals. The easiest night diving is from a boat.

CHAPTER III OAHU

OAHU AT A GLANCE

Although Oahu is the third largest of the Hawaiian Islands with an area of 608 square miles, it is home to more than three quarters of a million people, or about 80 percent of the total population of Hawaii.

The island is comprised of two greatly eroded shield volcanoes, now called the Waianae Range to the west and the Koolau Mountains to the east. Lava which flowed from these two volcanoes joined together to form the Leilehua Plateau in the center of the island. Pineapple and sugarcane fields now cover a large portion of this plateau in central Oahu.

The windward east coast of Oahu receives heavy rainfall which has fostered the magnificent forests and jungles. This side of the island is lightly populated and dotted with small bays and picturesque fishponds.

To the west of the Waianae Range on the leeward side of Oahu, small towns and endless beaches line the arid Waianae coastline between Kaena Point and Barber's Point. On the rugged northwestern end of the island are world famous surfing sites, such as the Banzai Pipeline, know for their towering waves.

Waikiki, the best known of all the beaches in the Islands, is located in Honolulu and is the center of the thriving tourist industry. There are more than 35,000 hotel rooms along Waikiki.

Oahu, known as the gathering place, is a melting pot of peoples and cultures. Honolulu, the state's capital, is located on the southeastern coast. It is both the most populous city in the state and the headquarters for virtually all major commercial and industrial activities in Hawaii. Honolulu is also the site of one of the nation's busiest international airports and the location of Pearl Harbor.

Beautiful vistas along Nuuanu Pali Drive, before the Nuuanu Pali Overlook, offer scenic views of the windward side of the island.

Waikiki Beach, one of the most famous in the world, is a two-mile long, narrow stretch of sand lined with high-rise hotels. In the background is Diamond Head Crater.

WHERE TO STAY

Honolulu International Airport is approximately 20 minutes from downtown Waikiki. There are more than 100 hotels and apartment hotels in Waikiki. World class dining and an endless variety of entertainment can be found within walking distance of most hotels. The northern and western shores provide a few rural hotels for those who like the quiet of country living instead of the hustle and bustle of downtown Honolulu. Most dive operations provide pickup service at hotels, but a rental car is recommended for sightseeing and non-diving activities.

Many red slate-pencil urchins can be found in Hanauma Bay. Unlike the spiny variety, these urchins are harmless.

EXPLORING OAHU

A Loop Around Eastern Oahu

The quickest way to get a true flavor of the diversity of the whole island is to rent a car and drive the 40-mile, one and a half hour loop around eastern Oahu. This route takes you from **Waikiki** over the **Koolau Mountain Range**, down to the lush east coast and back to Waikiki via **Koko Head National Park** and **Diamond Head**. Set aside a half-day for this trip.

Drive west out of Waikiki on Ala Moana Boulevard. You will pass the huge, 50-acre **Ala Moana Shopping Center** unique for its variety of restaurants, and over 180 stores, the **Ward's Center** and **Ward's Warehouse** complex. Turn right onto Alakea Street, near the **Aloha Tower**. This famous landmark provides an excellent view of the harbor area. Stay on Alakea Street until it becomes Queen Emma Street and then follow signs to the Pali Highway (61), which rises into the **Nuuanu Valley** on the west slope of the Koolau Range.

About 11 miles outside of Honolulu, there is a turnoff to **Nuuanu Pali Lookout**, which provides a spectacular view of the windward side of the island, stretching from **Makapu'u Point** north to the end of **Kaneohe Bay**. This towering cliff was the sight of King Kamehameha's victory over the defenders of Oahu in 1795.

Once you reach the town of Kailua, turn right onto the Kalanianaole Highway (72) and drive toward the eastern tip of Oahu. The highway bends south, reaching the beach at Waimanalo.

Be sure to stop at the **Sea Life Park**, a great way to become acquainted with Hawaii's marine life. It features an oceanarium of more than 2,000 sea creatures, plus trained false killer whales, porpoises and penguins.

Also, stop at **Makapu'u Point** for a look at Molokai, 26 miles across the Kaiwi Channel. Nearby is **Sandy Beach**, one of Hawaii's finest bodysurfing spots. Across from the beach is a side road which leads up to **Koko Crater Botanical Gardens**. The highway continues along Koko Head, offering views of Lanai and Molokai. Watch for a turnout which will overlook the **Halona Blowhole**. Just past the blowhole is **Hanauma Bay**, one of Hawaii's best snorkeling spots. After the highway becomes a limited access freeway (H-1), exit at Kealaolu Avenue and drive toward the water. Turn right onto Kahala Avenue which winds around the base of the extinct crater, **Diamond Head**, and through miles of impressive residences. Kahala Avenue becomes Diamond Head Road before dropping back to Waikiki at Kapiolani Park.

Lobe coral thrives in shallow areas subjected to heavy wave action.

There is a wide selection of top-flight restaurants in the Waikiki/Honolulu area. The dress code here is somewhat more formal than the rest of the islands. Slacks and collared shirts are suggested for men and dresses for women. Two excellent, albeit expensive, seafood restaurants are **John Dominis** and **Nick's Fishmarket**. **Keo's Thai Cuisine** is also a favorite. For continental food, the **Swiss Inn** in the Nui Valley is very popular with the locals. An inexpensive Japanese restaurant which the locals also like is **Suehiro's** and, for authentic Hawaiian food, you should try **Ono Hawaiian Foods**.

Waiamea Bay Beach Park, on the north shore of Oahu, is probably the most famous surfing spot in the world. During the winter, incredibly large waves roll into the mouth of this pretty bay.

A Loop of Northern Oahu

You should allow a full day for this excursion, which covers about 85 miles in three and a half hours of driving time. Leave Waikiki by traveling west on Ala Moana Boulevard, which becomes Nimitz Highway 92. If you want to stop off at **Pearl Harbor**, curve off to the right onto King Kamehameha Highway (99), (15a exit) north of the Honolulu International Airport, avoiding the Highway 1 freeway, and take it less than two miles along the docks of Pearl Harbor's East Lochs to the turnoff marked with the **USS Arizona** sign. Shuttles leave from there to take you to a number of historical sites at this important military landmark.

If you have already seen Pearl Harbor and are heading to the north shore, take the H-1 freeway west and then drive north on the H-2 superhighway or Route 99, up through the center of Oahu. This route passes through miles of military land and pineapple fields, between the ridges of the **Waianae Range** on the left and the **Koolau Range** on the right.

The bottom-dwelling manybar goatfish, seen here foraging for food, usually travels alone. One of the larger species of goatfishes, it measures up to 12 inches in length.

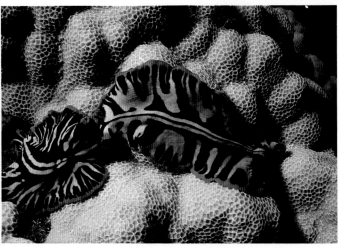

Flatworms are commonly seen on the vertical walls in the Ke'eau area. Although usually less than one inch in length, the flatworms pictured here are between two and three inches long.

At Wahiawa, H-2 ends and rural Oahu begins. Before continuing north on Route 99, stop at the **Dole Pineapple Pavillion** and the **Helemano Plantation** right up the road. About five miles of pineapple and sugarcane fields later, you will come to the seaside village town of Haleiwa. From Haleiwa, head northeast on the King Kamehameha Highway (83) toward **Kahuku Point** on Oahu's northeast tip. Along this 10-mile stretch, you will find Oahu's northern reefs and surfing beaches, including **Sunset Beach** (home of the **Banzai Pipeline**) and **Waimea Bay**. In the summer months, this area offers some terrific diving. In the winter months, plan to stop and watch surfers challenge the monster waves. Just inland from the bay is **Waimea Falls Park** with an 1,800-acre valley displaying a

beautiful waterfall, botanical gardens and nature trails.

Around the windy northeast point you will come to the **Amorient Aquafarm** just north of Kahuku, where varieties of shrimp, prawn and fish are raised. Near the town of Laie is the popular, 42-acre **Polynesian Cultural Center**, which offers simulated villages of seven Pacific islands. Between Laie and the town of Kaneohe, there is about 20 miles of tropical coastline, with tiny villages, palm-sheltered beaches, small farms and lush vegetation nestled against the vertical cliffs of the Koolau Mountains.

Just before you reach Kaneohe, take the Kahekili Highway (83) to the west, bypassing Kaneohe. On the outskirts of the town, in the **Valley of the Temples Memorial Park**, is the **Byodo-In Temple**, a precise replica of Japan's famed 900 year-old Kyoto temple, replete with Koi ponds, peacocks and gardens. Nearby is the **Haiku Gardens**, which offers an enchanting lily pond, acres of exotic plant life and a delightful, moderately-priced restaurant. The Kahekili Highway soon intersects with the Likelike Highway (63), which heads back through the Wilson Tunnel to Honolulu.

The Byodo-In Temple, located in the Valley of the Temples Memorial Park, is a precise replica of Japan's famous 900 year-old Kyoto Temple with Koi ponds, peacocks and gardens.

Up the Leeward Coast of Oahu

From Honolulu, you can visit Oahu's dry and sunny western coastline by going west on Route H-1 or Route 90. A half-day is enough time for this outing, unless you plan to stop for a picnic lunch and a swim at one of the beautiful leeward beaches. Visiting the sugarcane plantation town of **Ewa** is an interesting side trip. Turn off on exit 5a, which will put you on Route 76 heading south toward the coast. Near Oahu's southwest corner, Routes 99 and H-1 converge to become the Farrington Highway (93). This route heads north through an arid region appointed with rocky crags and cactus-studded hills to the towns of Waianae and Makaha. North from Makaha, near the **Kaena Point Satellite Tracking Station**, are some of the most beautiful yet sparsely populated beaches on the island.

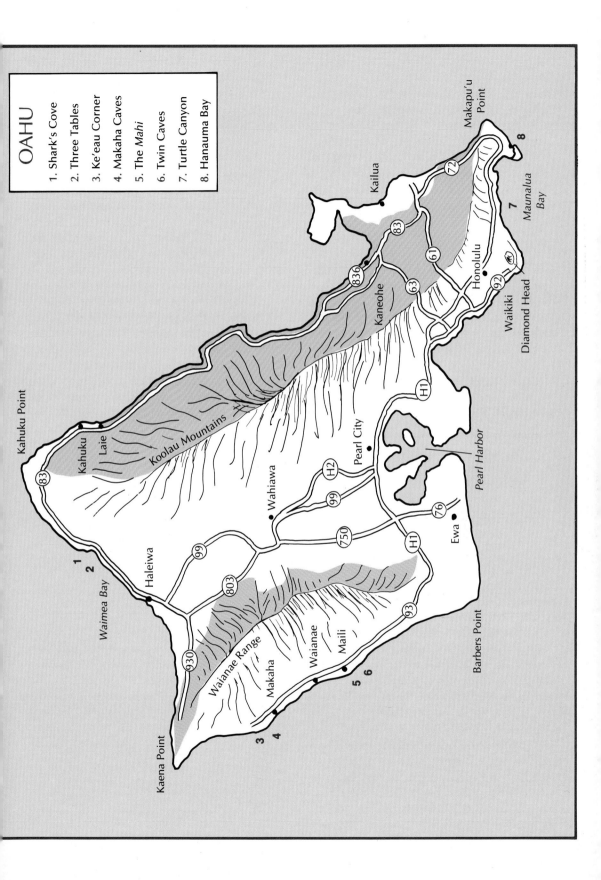

OAHU

1. Shark's Cove
2. Three Tables
3. Ke'eau Corner
4. Makaha Caves
5. The Mahi
6. Twin Caves
7. Turtle Canyon
8. Hanauma Bay

Diving on Oahu

Dive sites can be found on every side of Oahu. However, because of prevailing northeasterly trade winds and high north shore surf conditions during the winter, most diving occurs on Oahu's western and southeastern shores.

The major sites feature wrecks, large grottoes and colorful reef fishes. During the calm summer months, there are a number of interesting shore dives on the northern side of the island which are also very popular. Four harbors and additional launch facilities are located around the island which provide quick and easy access to a variety of sites, most of which are within a 30-minute boat ride. Oahu's dive stores are located throughout Honolulu and also in Hawaii Kai, Kailua, Kaneohe, Aiea, Makaha and Haleiwa. Some of the charter operations provide pickup service from the Waikiki hotels.

North Shore

1. SHARK'S COVE

DEPTH:	20-60 FEET
LEVEL:	NOVICE TO INTERMEDIATE
ACCESS:	SHORE

Shark's Cove is named after lava rocks which loosely resemble a shark. This area is primarily diveable during the calm summer months, but may also be accessible on exceptionally calm winter days.

Directions. Shark's Cove is located at Pupukea Beach Park on the north shore of Oahu. From Honolulu, take Highway 1 west. Turn right onto Highway 99 and drive north through the center of the island, past Wahiawa to Haleiwa on the northwest shore. Turn north (right) onto the coast road 83 for approximately 6 miles. Look for a large Foodland grocery store on the right past Waimea Bay and Waimea Falls. There is parking for Shark's Cove on the left side of the road at Pupukea Park. Shark's Cove is

part of the Pupukea Marine Life District of Hawaii and scuba divers are not permitted to spear fish inside the cove. Facilities at Shark's Cove include restrooms, showers and a picnic area.

The Dive. Enter at the small sandy beach and swim around the point on the right side of the bay. The reef wall in this area is honeycombed with caves to explore. Beginning 30 to 40 yards from the beach in only 20 feet of water is an elaborate system of caves and caverns. Depths here range from 20 to 60 feet. Expect to find tame fish, eels, arches, lava tubes and other unusual rock formations. There is good snorkeling as well as scuba diving. When it is calm, this is also an excellent spot for a night dive. Return to the beach through the center of the bay.

Caution. This area can be very dangerous during periods of medium to high surf. Stay out of the caves when there is any appreciable wave action. The area is almost always diveable from May to October but, during the winter months it is usually too rough.

Jim Robinson explores the interior hold of the Mahi *on the leeward shore of Oahu. The most well-known artificial reef in the Islands, this 165-foot minesweeper was intentionally sunk in 1983.*

2. THREE TABLES

DEPTH:	15-60 FEET
LEVEL:	INTERMEDIATE TO ADVANCED
ACCESS:	SHORE

This site has been named Three Tables because of three flat sections of lava rock which protrude just above the surface about 20 yards from shore.

Directions. Three Tables is located on the northern coast of Oahu, less than one mile southeast of Shark's Cove. Take Highway 1 west out of Honolulu and turn north onto Highway 99 up through the middle of the island. Turn right at Haleiwa and continue north on Highway 83 past Waimea Bay. About six miles from Haleiwa, you will come to a small parking area on the shore side of the road. The site should be readily recognizable by the three flat sections of rock.

The Dive. Access is from a small, sand beach or from the rocky shoreline in front of the parking area. Divers must use caution getting in and out of the water because of the wave action. Three tables is diveable throughout most of the summer months.

The depths increase along a gently sloping, rocky bottom from about 15 feet around the "tables" to about 60 feet. The large lava formations which lie directly offshore provide small caves and ledges to explore, but some of the better diving is to the right of the beach. About 150 yards offshore in approximately 60 feet of water is a maze of lava tubes, ledges and overhangs. This is an excellent area for macro photography, offering a variety of nudibranchs, crustaceans and other invertebrates, as well as a large number of eels. Divers will also find a wide variety of colorful reef fishes.

3. KE'EAU CORNER

DEPTH:	30-70 FEET
LEVEL:	NOVICE TO INTERMEDIATE
ACCESS:	BOAT

Ke'eau Corner is an extensive drop-off reef that runs from Makaha Caves to Ke'eau Beach Park. The top of the wall is in 30 feet of water and drops to a sand and rubble bottom 70 feet deep. There is normally very little current along the reef.

Spectacular lava formations adorn the walls of the seemingly endless canyons which run perpendicular to shore. The canyon walls are riddled with massive holes, tunnels and archways, forming a swiss cheese effect. In addition, numerous vertical columns can be found here. Look for long, white antennae of large, banded shrimp protruding from small cracks and recesses inside the columns.

The rubble at the bottom of the wall is an excellent place to find empty cowry and cone shells. The usual variety of tropicals, including moorish idols, triggerfish and various wrasses are present. Small white-mouth morays are frequently discovered poking their heads from beneath clumps of coral and from small openings in the lava.

Although Ke'eau Corner is primarily a boat dive, it can be reached from the rocky area or sandy beach at Ke'eau Beach Park after a very long swim.

Ke'eau Corner is an interesting reef site with its numerous large lava archways and tunnels.

4. MAKAHA CAVES

DEPTH:	20-45 FEET
LEVEL:	NOVICE TO INTERMEDIATE
ACCESS:	BOAT

The Makaha Caves or Caverns are located off Oahu's western shore. This is an excellent area for exploring lava caves, grottoes and ledges. On a nice day, the sunlight streams through the maze of openings in the tunnels, arches and overhangs where divers can find moorish idols, menpachi squirrelfish, puffers, hawkfish and other tropicals. Triggerfishes, including Hawaii's state fish, the Humuhumunukunukuapau'a, appear everywhere over the reef. In these shallower areas which contain the more interesting lava formations, there are also many schools of goatfish and blue-striped snapper. Divers will often see whitetip reef sharks lying on the sandy bottom in deep crevices.

Green turtles are often found near the sand in about 45 feet of water close to the outer edges of the reef. Because dive boats regularly use this site, the turtles are not as skittish as usual and will often allow divers to observe them from close range. The outer reef areas are often visited by schools of large, scrawled filefish and rudderfishes. Occasionally manta rays are seen here.

The Makaha Caves is an ideal area for a night dive. At night, divers will commonly see all kinds of nudibranchs including the large, bright red Spanish dancer. Spiny lobsters and the hairy Hawaiian lobster are often encountered in cracks and crevices, along with conger eels and green head eels. Blue, scrawled filefish, parrotfishes, goatfishes and other tropicals will often be encountered sleeping in recesses. Noticeably absent are the nocturnal blue-striped snapper, which forage individually out on the sand at night and school for protection during the day.

5. THE *MAHI*

DEPTH:	95 FEET
LEVEL:	INTERMEDIATE
ACCESS:	BOAT

The *Mahi* is a 165-foot minesweeper resting upright with her bow pointing seaward. The ship was sunk in 1983 to create an artificial reef and she now lies fully intact in 95 feet of water. Lying about a mile offshore from Maili Point, she has quickly become the most popular dive on the leeward side of the island.

The wreck is now inhabited by a wide variety of marine animals. Moray eels, including two 5-foot yellow margins, seem to inhabit every pipe and hole on the aft decks. A school of ravenous lemon yellow butterflyfish instantly greet each new team of divers that come down the mooring line. Schools of goatfish and blue-striped snapper hover around the perimeter of the hull.

Divers can easily penetrate inside the wreck when it is calm, exploring the pilothouse and three lower decks. They should, however, maintain proper buoyancy and stay off the bottom in order to keep from stirring up silt. In the interior, divers will discover menpachi, longjaw squirrelfish, bigeye squirrelfish, spiny lobsters, slipper lobsters and a wide variety of other animals, including the resident whitetip reef shark. The outside of the hull is literally covered with pipe cleaner nudibranchs.

When the visibility exceeds 100 feet, divers can see the large barge located off the port side of the *Mahi*. Only experienced divers should attempt to swim over to the barge and only when there is little or no current. Small eagle rays and an occasional manta ray visit the wreck.

Jim Robinson and Gene Clark are joined by a small school of curious milletseed butterflyfish on the deck of the Mahi. Butterflyfishes are one of the many types of reef fishes that congregate on this wreck.

6. TWIN CAVES

DEPTH:	45-110 FEET
LEVEL:	ADVANCED
ACCESS:	BOAT

This area is characterized by an impressive drop-off which wraps around Maili Point some distance from shore. The top of the wall is between 45 and 50 feet, dropping vertically to 80 or 90 feet, where there is a gentle slope to a flat sand and rubble bottom at 110 feet.

Because of the frequency of strong currents and the long distance from shore, this site must be visited by boat. Although the coral is relatively sparse in this area, there is an interesting and diverse assortment of marine life. Eagle and manta rays are occasionally seen here. Yellow margin, zebra, green head and white-mouth morays are all fairly common in the rubble areas at the bottom of the drop-off.

The site gets its name from two vertical lava tube columns. The southern column is entered at the end of a box canyon, through a large archway off to the right side. The northern column is entered by means of a low tunnel at the end of a second canyon. Look for pufferfish and varieties of squirrelfish hiding in crevices and under overhangs.

The drop-off is covered with pipe cleaner nudibranchs measuring up to 7 inches, as well as numerous other varieties. Tiny sabre-tooth blennies are plentiful. They mimic the actions of cleaner wrasses to attract fishes and then, instead of cleaning parasites, bite a chunk of flesh from their surprised victims.

Caution. Special care should be exercised at this site because of the depth and current.

A diver hovers above one of the vertical columns at Twin Caves on the leeward coast of Oahu. This site is characterized by an impressive drop-off.

7. TURTLE CANYON

DEPTH:	20-35 FEET
LEVEL:	INTERMEDIATE
ACCESS:	BOAT

Turtle canyon is located in Maunalua Bay on the southeast coast of Oahu. The reef is 20 to 35 feet deep, with a series of ridges that continue for an area of about a half-mile. The site is aptly named for the large number of green sea turtles which frequent this area. Divers can expect to see 5 to 10 turtles on any given dive. Turtles will usually be found resting on the sand or in depressions in the coral. The turtles here are so used to seeing divers that they will often completely ignore their presence, making this one of the easiest places in the world to get good turtle photographs.

There is also an extensive variety of other types of marine life on this reef. Schools of durgeons flock to the divers as they enter the water. The rubble and sandy sections around the perimeter of the reef provide excellent areas to find octopus, scorpionfishes, eels and shells. Tropicals, including triggerfishes, moorish idols and wrasses, and the four-spot, tear-drop and ornate butterflyfish are common.

Aside from the large population of turtles at Turtle Canyon, divers will also find octopuses, scorpionfishes, eels and a number of tropicals such as butterflyfishes and triggerfishes.

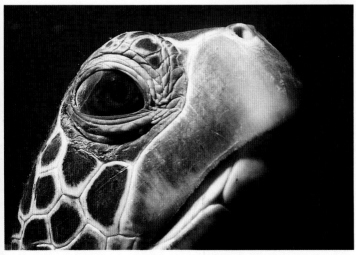

Turtles seem to be everywhere at the Turtle Canyon site on the south shore of Oahu. Divers can expect to see 5 to 10 turtles on any given dive.

Hanauma Bay is one of Oahu's prettiest and most popular beaches. The bottom of the bay is a maze of coral, providing excellent snorkeling year-round.

8. HANAUMA BAY

DEPTH:	10-100 FEET
LEVEL:	NOVICE TO ADVANCED
ACCESS:	SHORE, EXCELLENT SNORKELING

This breathtakingly beautiful bay is an extinct volcano, formed when the outer wall was breached by the sea. The bay opens southeasterly toward the sea and the inner edge of the bay is bordered by a sandy beach.

Directions. Located on Oahu's southeastern tip near Koko Head, Hanauma Bay is only a 20-minute drive from Waikiki Beach. Take highway 1 east out of Honolulu along the coast past Diamond Head and Koko Head Marina. At the top of Nonoula Crater, on Koko Head Ridge Road, you will see a sign on the right for Hanauma Bay. From the top of Koko Head, a side road and path lead down to the Bay.

Facilities include parking, showers, picnic tables, restrooms and concession stands. Lifeguards are on duty. Hanauma Bay gets very crowded, so it is advisable to dive early in the day.

Inner Reef. (Novice) The area inside the protecting reef is almost always calm and offers a good, safe area for swimming and snorkeling. The maximum depth is 10 feet or shallower. The fish in this area are tame and follow divers around for a handout.

Outer Reef. (Intermediate) Stay away from the outer reef when large southeast swells are present which happens only a few times a year. Depths range from 15 feet to 70 feet near the mouth of the bay. To reach the outer reef from shore, follow the large cable which runs through a channel leading to the reef. It can be found directly out from where the lifeguard chair is normally situated. Ask one of the lifeguards for directions. Follow the cable to find your way back to the inner reef.

Witch's Brew. (Advanced) The Witch's Brew is located just outside of the small peninsula which extends into the right-hand side of the bay. This area is called the Witch's Brew because wave action and current patterns merge here, causing turbulent surface water and strong surge underwater. In front of the peninsula is a lush coral reef along with rock ledges and abundant marine life.

Palea Point. (Advanced) The north tip of Hanauma Bay is known as Palea Point where there is a wall that drops from 15 to 100 feet. This site has an abundance of invertebrates. Many large fish frequent the area and sightings of turtles, eels and rays are not uncommon.

Caution. The current can get quite strong outside the mouth of the bay.

CHAPTER IV MAUI

MAUI AT A GLANCE

Maui is the second largest of the Hawaiian Islands, encompassing almost 729 square miles. The island is made up of two separate volcanoes connected in the middle by a low strip of land. The younger is Haleakala on the east, which rises to 10,023 feet. It is a huge, dormant shield volcano that has a massive crater at the top. The last time Haleakala erupted was about 1790. The slopes of the older volcano, now the West Maui Mountains, have been severely eroded leaving numerous valleys and peaks. These lush mountains are only about half as high as Haleakala and receive more rainfall than any other place in the world except for parts of nearby Kauai.

The isthmus, or lowland, was formed by lava flowing together from these two volcanoes. This lowland area contains some of the most productive soil on the island as well as the largest concentration of people.

The island's commercial and civic centers are located in the northern cities of Kahului and Wailuku. These cities are on the windy side of the island where the seas are usually rough. The western shores of Maui are the leeward side of the island, and it is here that the waters are calm and clear, ideal for scuba diving. The islands of Lanai and Molokai lie directly across the straits from the leeward side of Maui.

Tourism is now the major industry on Maui and the majority of tourists select West Maui as their base while visiting the island. The resort areas of Kaanapali and Wailea are sheltered from significant rainfall by the bulk of the protective mountains. The center of the dive industry on Maui is in Lahaina, just to the south of Kaanapali. An historic town, Lahaina was the center of the whaling industry in Hawaii as well as the original capital of the Hawaiian Kingdom. There are also several dive operations further south in the more recently developed communities of Kihei and Wailea.

The Iao Needle, a verdant peak which rises 2,250 feet at the head of the Iao Valley, is one of Maui's most famous landmarks. This valley is known for its beautiful paths, cool streams and scenic views.

The West Maui Mountains
provide a lush backdrop for the
variety of water activities
available in Lahaina. Parasailing
is an adventurous way to get a
bird's eye view of the harbor.

In the early 1800's, Lahaina was
a wild and colorful whaling
port. Today, it is the
commercial center for the
tourist industry, offering a wide
array of water-related sports
including scuba diving and
sportfishing.

GETTING THERE

The only airport on Maui which is currently able to service jet planes is the main airport at Kahului, only 25 minutes flying time from Honolulu. Kahului is located on the northeast side of the isthmus. Mainland visitors can fly here directly from the West Coast on United or American Airlines. Aloha Airlines, Hawaiian Airlines and Reeves Air provide connecting flights with other islands.

The West Maui Kapalua Airport, located several miles north of Lahaina, is now open on a limited basis, bringing tourists into the Lahaina/Kaanapali area. Also, there is a short landing strip at Hana on Maui's lush northeastern corner. Only the small Princeville Airlines flies into this isolated community.

Maui offers divers a wide variety of living accommodations. The Plantation Inn, a ''bed and breakfast'' located in the heart of Lahaina, caters to divers.

WHERE TO STAY

Most visitors to Maui elect to stay on the west side of the island which is where most of the resort development and almost all of the dive stores and dive boat operations are located. For convenience, visiting divers should select lodging on the west coast.

The Kaanapali Beach Resort, with seven condominiums and six hotels, is located on a 1,200-acre site which fronts a long, sandy beach area north of Lahaina. This area has become a model for similar projects in Hawaii and elsewhere around the world. Further to the north, quite a number of low-rise condominiums and a few large hotels line the beaches at Honokowai, Kahana, Napili Bay and Kapalua Bay.

To the south of the central isthmus, there are more than forty-five condominiums, many of them high-rises, packed along the sandy beaches in Kihei. Down the road in Wailea, there are only two luxury hotels and a few low-rise condominiums in an area three times the size of Waikiki. South of Wailea, there is yet another resort community in Makena.

EXPLORING MAUI

Maui is only 48 miles from its eastern to western tip, but it offers more varied drive excursions than any of the other islands. The best way to explore Maui is to take short drives to different parts of the island. A circular trip around the island is not recommended because the roads on the north end and south end are unimproved and, in places, passage can be difficult or even hazardous.

End of the Road in West Maui

A good way to begin is with a half-day driving excursion of western Maui at the **Iao Valley**. To get there from the Lahaina area, simply take Highway 30 back to Wailuku on the northeast side of the island. Drive through the old Wailuku District until you come to a stop sign. Turn left and follow the signs for the **Iao Needle**.

This is the site of the battle of Kepaniwai, where King Kamehameha conquered Maui in 1790, by trapping its army in the steep-sided **Iao Valley**. Above the jungled head of the valley rises the 2,250 foot peak called the **Iao Needle**. Take time to stroll along the paths and cool off in the streams.

After coming back down the Iao Valley road, turn right (south) onto the Honoapiilani Highway 30 at mile marker '0' and proceed across Maui's low lying central plain through thousands of acres of sugarcane fields. Haleakala will be on your left and the West Maui Mountains on your right. On the right hand side, you will see the **Maui Tropical Plantation**. Here you can take a tram through orchards and groves displaying dozens of varieties of island fruits. You can also visit the museum, tropical nursery and aquaculture exhibit.

Stay on Highway 30 past the Maalaea Bay boat harbor. The road will swing to the northwest as you reach the coast. There are excellent lookout points along the highway over the next several miles. Stop at the scenic lookout near the lighthouse at **McGregor Point**. The island straight ahead is Kahoolawe and the one to the right is Lanai. The highway drops back down to sea level just before you get to the tiny village of **Olowalu**.

Olowalu is the site of **Chez Paul**, an unlikely spot for one of two excellent French restaurants on Maui. The long stretch of beach south of Olowalu has excellent shallow water snorkeling. When it is clear at **Hekili Point**, you can view four of the other islands: Molokai, Lanai, Kahoolawe and Hawaii.

As you approach **Lahaina**, the road edges away from the coast. Several turnoffs will take you into the laid-back downtown area. Lahaina's main streets offer numerous shops, galleries, boutiques, restaurants, historical sites and, of course, numerous dive stores and charter operations. A large number of fishing charters also leave out of Lahaina.

Follow Front Sreet along the water and it will eventually merge with the Honoapiilani Highway heading north. Lahaina has a number of top-rated restaurants including **Gerard's** (French), **Longhi's** (Italian) and the **Chart House** (seafood).

To the north of Lahaina is the resort community of **Kaanapali**, and the resort towns of Kahana, Napili and Kapalua. **Whaler's Village** is an extensive shopping complex within the Kaanapali area. Beyond Kapalua, the developed areas come to an abrupt end. Along this undeveloped shoreline are a number of hidden beaches, including the picturesque **Honolua Bay**.

Most boat charters offer two or three tank dives, allowing divers to visit a number of different locations in a day. Here, a diver takes the opportunity to snorkel between dives.

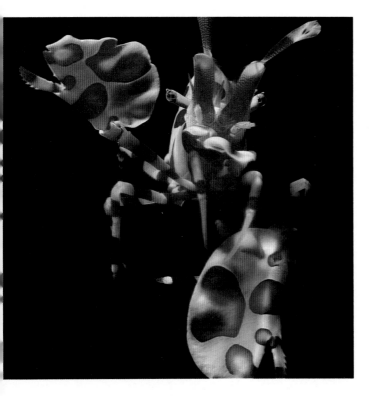

Hawaii's waters are home to many rare and unique creatures. This tiny harlequin shrimp has become scarce, partly because of the demand by amateur aquarists. Its gaudy appearance makes it one of the most sought-after marine animals for photographers as well as collectors.

To Haleakala and the Ulupalakua Ranch

A must-see for any visitor to Maui is **Mt. Haleakala**, which rises nearly two miles above sea level, and its crater, which measures twenty-one miles around. Be sure to set aside a full day for this trip, especially if you plan to tour the crater itself.

Take the **Haleakala Highway** (37) out of Kahului through miles of pineapple and sugarcane fields. At Pulalani, turn left and head east, staying on the Haleakala Highway which changes to 377. The highway will swing to the south, taking you through upland meadows and stands of eucalyptus trees. In six miles, you will reach the uphill turnoff to the left for the 22-mile **Haleakala Crater Road** (378). Flower farms line the road on the climb. The **Kula Lodge**, located just before the turnoff to the crater road, is a great place to stop for a meal and a scenic look at West Maui. The **Haleakala National Park Headquarters** is located at 7,000 feet, halfway up the switchback road to the edge of the crater. The views from the top, especially during the clear early morning hours, are incredible.

After coming back down the crater road, turn left onto the Haleakala Highway. Be sure to make a stop at the **Kula Botanical Gardens** which displays examples of native and tropical vegetation. A left turn at Kula Highway (37) will lead to **Ulupalakua**, a ranching settlement near the southern end of the island. To return to the Kahului area, turn around and drive north on Highway 37.

The Road to Hana

The 52-mile long, beautiful drive to Hana has over 600 curves and almost 60 bridges. The drive will usually take from three to four hours each way. Areas of dense tropical rain forest, waterfalls and bamboo thickets hug the side of the road along towering cliffs and deep ravines. The accommodations at Hana are limited but include the **Hana-Maui Hotel**, a luxury resort.

Waianapanapa State Park, with its black sand beach and fantastic sea caves, is located near the Hana District. Highway 31 continues past the small town of Hana for about ten miles. The several sites along this stretch include **Hamoa Beach, Wailua Falls** and the famed **Seven Sacred Pools**.

Over the past 25 years, Hawaii's pineapple industry has been reduced to only a few relatively small operations. Maui, however, still has substantial acreage devoted to growing this sweet fruit.

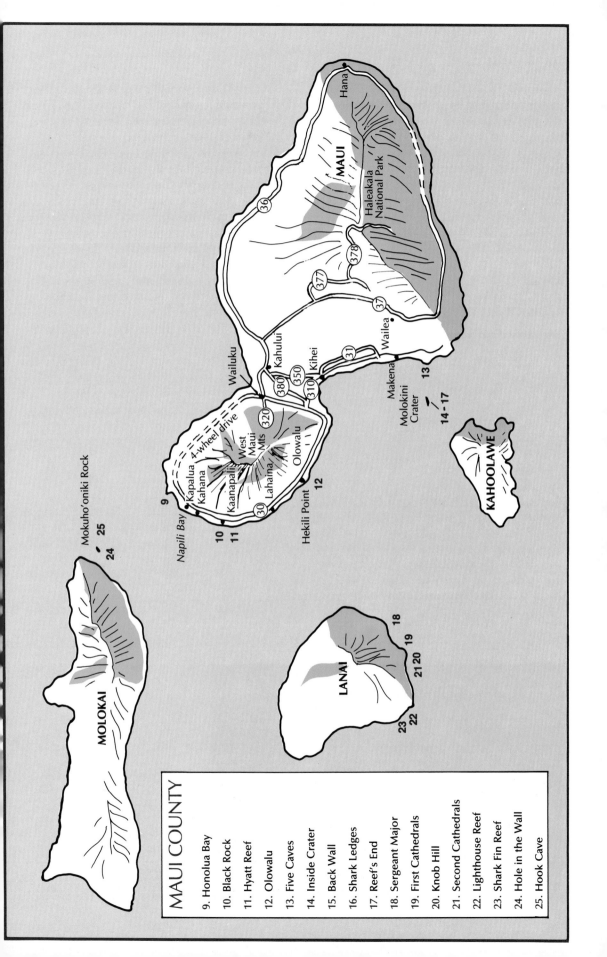

MAUI COUNTY

9. Honolua Bay
10. Black Rock
11. Hyatt Reef
12. Olowalu
13. Five Caves
14. Inside Crater
15. Back Wall
16. Shark Ledges
17. Reef's End
18. Sergeant Major
19. First Cathedrals
20. Knob Hill
21. Second Cathedrals
22. Lighthouse Reef
23. Shark Fin Reef
24. Hole in the Wall
25. Hook Cave

MOLOKAI

Mokuho'oniki Rock
25
24

MAUI

Hana

Haleakala
National Park

36
378
377
37

Wailuku
Kahului
Wailea
Makena
Molokini
Crater
Kihei
13
14–17

350
380
310
320
31

West
Maui
Mts
Olowalu

Kapalua
Kahana
4-wheel drive
Kaanapali
Lahaina
Napili Bay
Hekili Point
30
9
10
11
12

LANAI

18
19
21 20
23
22

KAHOOLAWE

DIVING MAUI

The island of Maui offers excellent diving all year round along its leeward western shore. The contour of the coastline provides for protected areas even during the most severe winter swells. Dive charters leave on a daily basis from Lahaina, Kihei and Maalaea Harbor for inter-island trips to Molokini Crater and Lanai, as well as to popular sites along the leeward side of Maui. There are also occasional trips to the nearby islands of Molokai and Kahoolawe.

MAUI

9. HONOLUA BAY

DEPTH:	5-50 FEET
LEVEL:	NOVICE TO INTERMEDIATE
ACCESS:	SHORE

Honolua Bay is a beautiful secluded spot on the northwest tip of Maui.

Directions. Drive north from Lahaina on coastal Highway 30 past the communities of Napili and Kapalua and the beaches of Fleming and Slaughterhouse (Mokuleia) and you will be overlooking a U-shaped bay with a rock and sand beach at its base. Park your car at the bottom of the hill and walk about a quarter mile down the dirt road to the bay.

The Dive. Honolua Bay is a popular spot for introductory and night dives. It is a great site for snorkelers as well because of the beautiful areas of coral whose tops come within 5 feet of the surface. The corals are most abundant on the north side of the bay. Many of the fish are quite tame due to the marine preserve status of the bay.

Among the myriad cracks and crevices to explore, abundant reef fishes, including schools of goatfishes, butterflyfishes, surgeonfishes, wrasses, triggerfishes, eels, puffers and moorish idols can be seen. The middle of the bay is sandy but look for the arches near the entrance to the bay on the left. At the bay's mouth is a drop-off to 50 feet. Here, large pelagics are often seen including manta rays, kahala, barracuda and ulua. The bay is also a popular boat dive site and when diving the middle of the bay, one should be mindful of boat traffic. Diving is best during the spring and summer; in the fall and winter it is a popular surfing site.

Large antler corals thrive off the west coast of Maui and are home to a variety of crabs, fishes and shrimp.

Hermit crabs are commonly seen on night dives. They usually have large colorful eyes and make excellent subjects for photographers.

10. BLACK ROCK

DEPTH:	20-30 FEET
LEVEL:	NOVICE
ACCESS:	SHORE OR BOAT

Black Rock is a huge lava formation that serves as the foundation for the Sheraton Hotel on Kaanapali Beach.

Directions. Drive north out of Lahaina on Highway 30 until you see the Kaanapali Resort entrance. Turn left into the complex and follow the road around to the right until you get to the Sheraton. There is a small public parking lot at the north end of the hotel. Enter the water on the north side of Black Rock. There is also a public beach access just past the Kaanapali Beach Hotel, about a 150-yard walk to the beach. For day dives, it may be easier to arrange for snorkeling or scuba rentals at the Sheraton or Kaanapali Beach Hotel. You may be able to obtain a permit for parking by contacting hotel management in advance.

The Dive. This is primarily a shore dive with easy access and sandy beach entries and exits. Depths range from 20 to 30 feet. While most of the beach is sand, the black volcanic rock peninsula juts out several hundred feet from shore and it is here you will find the best visibility and marine life. This rock peninsula offers a protective cove that is excellent for novice divers and provides easy navigation for night dives. By diving along the cinder cone, you can easily keep your bearings and concentrate on the many holes in the volcanic rock where you will find a great variety of creatures. Be attentive to boat traffic and aware that swimmers use some of the rock outcroppings as jumping platforms.

Black Rock, a huge lava formation, located at the Sheraton Hotel on Kaanapali Beach, is popular as a night dive. It has easy entry and exit points as well as a wide variety of marine life. Spanish dancer nudibranchs are often seen here.

Green turtles are seen on almost every dive at Hyatt Reef. Their large oval, greenish-brown shells blend in well with the tops of coral. During the day they can be seen rising to the surface to gulp air.

11. HYATT REEF

DEPTH:	40-60 FEET
LEVEL:	NOVICE TO INTERMEDIATE
ACCESS:	BOAT

The Hyatt Reef lies offshore from the Hyatt Regency Resort on Kaanapali Beach. Dive boats usually anchor near the outer edge of the reef in about 40 feet of water. The sandy bottom drops down to about 60 feet. Be sure to pay attention to the current at this site because it can become quite strong at times.

Along the outside of the coral runs a small ledge. The reef itself has densely packed coral formations which are cut by sand channels running perpendicular to the shoreline. Small eagle rays are frequently seen cruising in mid-water along the outer edge of the reef. A large variety of tropicals inhabit the area, including moorish idols, ornate butterflyfish, goatfishes, yellowtail coris and small trevally jacks. Divers also regularly encounter octopuses and small moray eels.

Green Sea Turtles. The major attraction at this site, however, is the abundance of large green sea turtles. Divers can usually count on seeing 8 to 10 turtles on a single excursion. The turtles blend in with the reef as they rest on top of the coral or in hollowed-out depressions. During the day they are active and can often be seen rising slowly to the surface to gulp air.

Some of the dive operators in Lahaina regularly visit this area on one-tank afternoon dives.

12. OLOWALU

DEPTH:	45 FEET
LEVEL:	NOVICE
ACCESS:	BOAT OR SHORE

Olowalu is an ideal place for snorkeling from the shore. For scuba diving, access is primarily by boat.

Directions. Drive south from Lahaina on Highway 30 until you come to a long stretch of narrow beach lining the roadway.

The Dive. This site remains very shallow for a long distance from shore, with coral heads coming up close to the surface. South swells or runoff from heavy rains can at times drastically reduce the visibility. However, when conditions are comparatively calm, visibility is good—up to 80 feet in offshore areas. Except for rare times when the surf is heavy, entries and exits from the two-mile long sandy beach are easy. Because of the extensive coral growth in this area, there is an exceptionally large number of tropicals to be found. The reef fishes include tangs, surgeonfishes, saddle wrasse, moorish idols, large hawkfish and butterflyfishes.

Green Sea Turtles. Turtles can often be found congregating along the reef that runs for several miles. The terrain is very similar throughout, with broken sand channels running perpendicular to shore.

Currents here are generally very mild to non-existent. Dive charter boats out of Lahaina frequently use this area for night dives.

Moray eels have a reputation for being ferocious. Their seemingly aggressive demeanor is a result of their need to continuously open and close their mouths to force water over their gills. Here, at the General Store at Olowalu, a whitemouth moray and a diver take a close look at each other.

13. FIVE CAVES

DEPTH:	40 FEET
LEVEL:	INTERMEDIATE TO ADVANCED
ACCESS:	SHORE

A small protected cove also known as the Five Graves and the Cemetery.

Directions. Drive south from Wailea on Wailea Alanui Drive, and turn right onto Makena Road just past the Makena Surf Condominiums. There is a dirt road at Nahuna Point, which leads to the water and the site of a small cemetery.

The Dive. Swim straight out through the natural channel and begin your dive past the wash rocks. On the north side of the reef, which runs perpendicular to the shoreline, are a series of caves in about 40 feet of water. Divers are likely to run into a small, whitetip reef shark. There is also a good chance of seeing turtles. In almost every crack and crevice can be found Hawaiian bigeye and glasseye squirrelfish.

The best time to dive in this area is in the early morning when it is usually calm. If the surf is up, stay out of the water.

MOLOKINI CRATER

Crescent-shaped Molokini Crater is the tip of a small, extinct volcano which lies just off Makena on southwestern Maui. Only about a third of the crater rim, approximately 400 meters in length, still protrudes above water.

Charter boats from Kihei and Waalaea Bay visit the crater almost daily, and the large operations from Lahaina every few days. Morning is the best time to dive the crater because the afternoon winds cause the waves to increase in size.

Molokini is strictly a boat dive site. There are four distinct areas to scuba dive at Molokini and, in addition, the inside of the crater affords an excellent protected area for snorkelers. Molokini is a Marine Conservation District, so nothing may be taken or disturbed.

Molokini Crater, a crescent-shaped tip of a small, extinct volcano off southwestern Maui, offers a variety of dive sites. Divers will see an occasional branch of black coral protruding from a vertical wall along the back side of the crater.

14. INSIDE CRATER

DEPTH:	10-100 FEET
LEVEL:	NOVICE TO ADVANCED
ACCESS:	BOAT

This area is the most popular anchorage for dive boats visiting Molokini. The bottom on the inside slopes gradually from 30 feet to 100 feet. Some of the reef comes to within 10 feet of the surface making it an ideal snorkeling spot. Divers will find swarms of lemon butterflyfish, chubs, surgeonfishes, trumpetfishes, wrasses and other common reef fishes, as well as moray eels, and occasionally, manta rays and turtles.

15. BACK WALL

DEPTH:	TO 130+ FEET
LEVEL:	INTERMEDIATE TO ADVANCED
ACCESS:	BOAT

The back side of Molokini is a vertical wall which drops from the surface to a sand bottom at 350 feet. This is a drift dive, with the boat following the bubbles of the divers below. The entry point will depend upon which way the current is running. The sheer drop is spectacular and divers often see large pelagics, including yellowfin tuna, small gray sharks, trevally jacks, spinner dolphins and rays. The wall itself is not very colorful, but the undercuts and cracks are well worth exploring. On the wall, you will find black coral trees, lemon and raccoon butterflyfishes feeding on sergeant major eggs, and lots of nudibranchs.

16. SHARK LEDGES

DEPTH:	50-130+ FEET
LEVEL:	INTERMEDIATE TO ADVANCED
ACCESS:	BOAT

This site is at the northeastern tip of the crescent, on the side of the crater closest to Maui. There are a series of ledges ranging from 50 feet to 140 feet which are frequented by large but docile whitetip reef sharks. There are also a number of large, resident moray eels. This dive can be done as a deep dive or as the beginning of a drift dive along the wall.

17. REEF'S END

DEPTH:	80-120 FEET
LEVEL:	INTERMEDIATE TO ADVANCED
ACCESS:	BOAT

Dive boats also anchor inside the submerged extension of Molokini's northwest tip, an area which contains some of Molokini's most colorful corals.

Caution. All sites at Molokini, except those inside the crater, can experience strong currents. Also, because of the extreme depth in some areas, divers must monitor their gauges frequently to avoid dropping too deep.

On the inside of Molokini Crater, schools of tame fishes often swarm around divers looking for handouts. These lemon butterflyfish provide colorful subjects for photographers and interesting companions for divers.

Whitetip reef sharks are common at many sites in Hawaiian waters.

18. SERGEANT MAJOR

DEPTH:	40-50 FEET
LEVEL:	NOVICE
ACCESS:	BOAT

This reef was originally named because of the abundance of sergeant major fish which can be found in this area.

The main site consists of three parallel ridges perpendicular to shore. A long tunnel extends through one of the ridges and there are a host of caves to explore. A rippled sand channel separates the main site from two nearby parallel ridges called Sergeant Minor. A wide variety of tropicals inhabit these areas and one can expect to encounter at least one large green sea turtle.

19. FIRST CATHEDRALS

DEPTH:	40-60 FEET
LEVEL:	INTERMEDIATE
ACCESS:	BOAT

Puu Pehe Rock, also called First Cathedrals, is between Hulopoe Bay and Manele Bay on the southern shore of the island of Lanai. This area can be reached by charter boat from Maui and is diveable all year except when there is a southerly swell.

Huge Grotto. The main attraction is a huge underwater grotto full of lava formations including arches, caves, tubes, cracks, crevices and interconnecting passageways. The dive begins through a large, triangular archway at a depth of 40 feet. Continue swimming through a large tunnel which opens into a rear cavern. The cavern is given a cathedral-like appearance by flickering rays of light streaming through a latticework of holes and cracks in the rear wall. Schools of menpachi fill cracks and crevices on the sides of the main grotto.

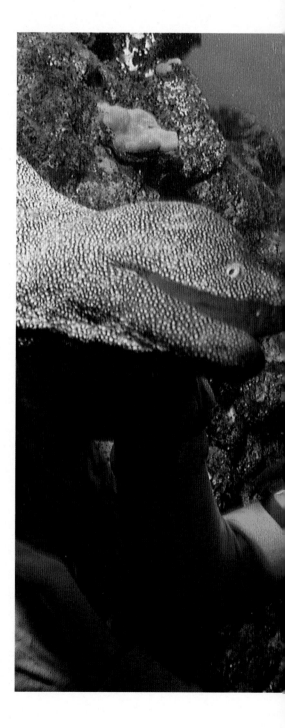

A number of eels at popular dive sites are used to being fed by dive guides. Here a whitemouth eel hopes for a handout from Julie Robinson.

Divers should take lights so that they can explore small side caves and crevices where it is common to find nudibranchs, lobsters, cowries and shrimp. There are several rear holes and tunnels which lead to the backside of the wash rock. In this area, divers will often see schools of pyramid butterflyfish, puffers, trumpetfish and blue-striped snappers.

When it is calm, the visibility often exceeds 100 feet. Maximum depths on the outside reach about 60 feet. Morning is the best time to dive, when the wind is minimal and the swells are at their smallest.

20. KNOB HILL

DEPTH:	15-70+ FEET
LEVEL:	INTERMEDIATE
ACCESS:	BOAT

Knob Hill is another popular dive site on the south shore of Lanai. The location is named after a huge lava rock which rises to within 15 feet of the surface. The rock is supported by leg formations which form caves and archways. There are usually one or two whitetip reef sharks which can be found resting at the bottom of these recesses.

Two ridges extend from this point and slope gradually into deeper water. Ledges and overhangs along the sides of these ridges are occupied by moray eels, octopuses and scorpionfishes. Crown-of-thorns sea stars are quite common in this area. Several schools of racoon butterflyfish roam about the reef.

Caution. When there is a southerly swell, this area can be very surgy.

21. SECOND CATHEDRALS

DEPTH:	15-65 FEET
LEVEL:	NOVICE TO INTERMEDIATE
ACCESS:	BOAT

Off the southern shore of Lanai is a massive, hollow pinnacle which rises from 65 feet to within 15 feet of the surface. This area is only diveable when the ocean is calm.

Cavernous Room. The main entrance to this pinnacle is found at its base on the ocean side. A large column splits the opening, allowing divers to enter on either side. The interior cavern consists of a gigantic room with several tunnels providing rear exits. Although the inside appears fairly barren at first glance, divers using a light to explore interior cracks and crevices will be well rewarded. Cowries, nudibranchs, lobsters, moray eels, menpachi and crabs can be found throughout the interior. A large tree of soft coral can be found protruding from the ceiling.

Swarms of fishes, including schools of pyramid butterflyfish and durgeons, cluster around the top of the pinnacle. Toward the end of the dive, air bubbles which have filtered up through the ceiling percolate through the coral-encrusted top of the pinnacle.

The Second Cathedrals is a network of caverns and tunnels within a huge underwater pinnacle which rises to within 15 feet of the surface. A variety of marine life can be found hiding among the cracks and crevices.

22. LIGHTHOUSE REEF

DEPTH:	20-60 FEET
LEVEL:	NOVICE TO INTERMEDIATE
ACCESS:	BOAT

This site off the southwest tip of Lanai, is named for a small, white, unmanned lighthouse that sits on the point. The conditions in this location are almost always calm because the reef is protected by a natural breakwater jutting from the point.

On the side of the ridge where dive boats usually anchor is a vertical wall that drops to a gently sloping coral and rubble bottom in 30 feet of water. At the bottom of the wall is a small archway that provides an excellent setting for photographing diver models.

A long lava tube at Lighthouse Reef offers a variety of interesting invertebrates. The back wall of the tube is crowded with candy cane shrimp.

Lava Tubes. After leaving the arch, follow the base of the wall to the right until you come to the first of two lava tubes. The first is usually inhabited by at least one, and sometimes three, small, whitetip reef sharks. The second tube is about 12 feet in diameter and 60 feet deep. Hawaiian lobsters will frequently be seen in crevices along the sides of the tube. The back wall is literally covered with hundreds of 'candy-cane' shrimp.

Caution. The bottom of the tube is covered with fine silt which, when stirred up, can reduce visibility drastically. Penetrating this tube requires use of a light and should be left to advanced divers only.

Away from the wall, the bottom slopes off into sand, boulders and rubble. Pufferfishes, surgeonfishes, moray eels, Hawaiian turkeyfish and schools of pennantfish are fairly common in this area.

Caution. Stay away from the point, where the currents can become quite strong.

Shark Fin Reef, located just north of Lighthouse Reef, is named after the lava rock protruding from the water which resembles a shark's fin.

23. SHARK FIN REEF

DEPTH:	20-70 FEET
LEVEL:	INTERMEDIATE
ACCESS:	BOAT

Shark Fin is so named because the ridge which sticks out of the water resembles the dorsal fin of a shark. The site is located just to the north of Lighthouse Reef, on the southwest tip of Lanai. The preferred anchorage for dive boats is in a sandy area 40 feet deep, just to the northeast of the ridge. The average depth of this dive runs from 20 feet on the inside to over 70 feet on the outer edge of the ridge.

Upon entering the water, divers are immediately greeted by schools of aggressive rudderfishes, black durgeons and milletseed butterflyfish. There is an archway at the inner side of the ridge in about 20 feet of water through which divers can swim. Large pelagics, such as rays and jacks, are occasionally seen in blue water off the end of the ridge.

There is a parallel ridge to the south and a small, submerged pinnacle with three caves on the shore side. The shallows are a good place to finish the dive because the fish are used to being fed. Scorpionfishes, octopuses and various small morays are regularly encountered on the rubble bottom.

MOLOKAI: MOKUHO'ONIKI ROCK

A few of the dive operators on Maui run occasional trips to Mokuho'oniki Rock, at the east end of Molokai. Prevailing winds and ocean conditions allow this excursion to be run only about 25 days out of the year. The marine life found in this area is unusual and exciting. Hammerhead sharks, eagle rays, barracuda, large jacks and manta rays are often seen here along the drop-offs.

Large pelagics, such as manta rays, eagle rays and hammerhead sharks often appear along the drop-off at Mokuho'oniki. This site is accessible only about 25 days out of the year because of wind and water conditions.

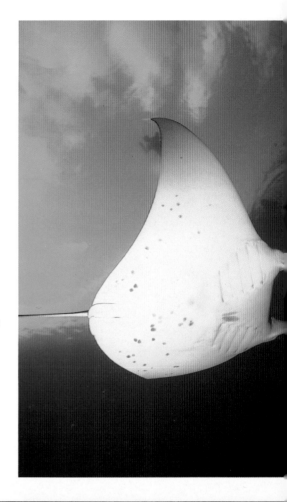

A school of squirrelfish swim inside the many holes and crevices at the First Cathedrals.

24. HOLE IN THE WALL

DEPTH:	20-100 FEET
LEVEL:	ADVANCED
ACCESS:	BOAT

The reef here drops off to a gently sloping sand and rubble bottom in about 100 feet of water. On the west side of the reef, there is a razor-edged ridge which drops off vertically on either side. Usually, a strong current rips over the top of the area. Many large tropicals take refuge from the current beneath ledges near the top of the ridge. Large schools of goatfishes, pennantfish, pyramid butterflyfish and blue-striped snapper are found between 20 to 40 feet. Foot-long titan scorpionfish are fairly common here.

A diver swims with a school of goatfish at Mokuho'oniki off the southeastern point of Molokai. An unusually large number of schooling fishes frequent this site.

25. HOOK COVE

DEPTH:	20-100 FEET
LEVEL:	ADVANCED
ACCESS:	BOAT

This site is a huge, semi-circular bowl whose walls slope upward gently from a depth of 40 feet to a jumble of boulders in the shallows. The nearby drop-off falls to well below 100 feet. Large pelagics, such as barracuda, rays and hammerhead sharks often cruise up over the wall. Throughout the shallows around the bowl are swarms of tropicals. There are some excellent spots for sighting octopuses here.

Abundant Lobsters. As a night dive, this area will invariably produce an incredible assortment of nocturnal creatures. Lobsters are usually found in abundance, along with large tiger cowries, triton's trumpets, Spanish dancer nudibranchs, octopuses, moray eels, puffers and varieties of scorpionfishes.

CHAPTER V HAWAII

The Big Island

THE BIG ISLAND AT A GLANCE

The "Big Island" of Hawaii makes up almost two-thirds of the entire land area of the state of Hawaii. The island was formed by five shield volcanoes. Of these five, Mauna Loa (13,677 feet) and Kilauea (4,093 feet) are still active. The size of the island and the range of elevations are responsible for very different climate zones in different parts of the island. The windward coast is very windy and receives considerable precipitation. The Kona Coast, which is the west or leeward side, is shielded from the trade winds and is very dry most of the year.

Despite its size, the "Big Island" is only lightly populated. Because it is a relatively young island geologically, Hawaii has few sandy beaches. Large areas of agricultural land south of Hilo on the east coast are devoted to growing orchids, arthuriums, papayas and macadamia nuts.

Tourist development is centered around Kailua-Kona, where one will find most of the dive stores and dive boat operations. There is a growing number of quality hotels and condominiums along the dry, sunny Kona and Kohala coasts. Excellent package prices are available which include lodging, airfare and diving.

Akaka Falls State Park, north of Hilo, is a "must-see" on any tour of the windward side of the Big Island. A nature trail leads past bamboo groves, ferns and colorful orchids to a scenic view of the 420-foot Akaka Falls.

The resort town of Kailua is the business and shopping center of the Kona Coast, featuring hotels, restaurants and more shopping malls per square mile than almost anywhere else in the Islands.

GETTING THERE

There are four airports on the Big Island. The main facility is the Keahole Airport, located on the Kona Coast about 9 miles north of Kailua-Kona. Many visitors take advantage of the convenient direct flights offered by United Airlines from selected mainland cities. This airport is also served by Aloha Airlines, Hawaiian Airlines and Princeville Airways, which provide inter-island flights. General Lyman Field is located on the east side of the island in Hilo. This airport is also served by the large inter-island carriers. Both of these airports have a cafeteria, cocktail lounge and gift shops.

The other two facilities, Upolu Airport on the northwest Kohala Peninsula and Waimea-Kohala Airport near the town of Waimea on the Parker Ranch, are little more than landing fields and are used only by propeller-driven aircraft.

Outrigger canoe trips set sail from a beautiful little beach next to the King Kamehameha Hotel. Located inside the marina in Kailua-Kona, the calm water provides a perfect site for a relaxing swim.

WHERE TO STAY

There are three main resort areas on the island of Hawaii. The island's major luxury resorts are located on the Kohala Coast and the northern Kona Coast. One of the newest of these self-contained resorts is the Hyatt Regency Waikoloa on the Kohala Coast, which was opened in late 1988.

Most Big Island hotels and condominiums are concentrated in Hilo and Kailua-Kona. A limited amount of lodging can also be found scattered in outlying areas all around the island. The Kona Coast, from Keauhou Bay to Kailua-Kona, and the Kohala Coast to the north have developed into the Big Island's resort destination areas. Because the diving charters on Hawaii operate principally out of the Kailua Harbor and Honokohau Harbor on the Kona Coast, it is most convenient for visiting divers to stay in this area.

EXPLORING THE BIG ISLAND

The island of Hawaii is usually perceived as having two distinct sides, the Kona side and the Hilo side. Hilo, which is located on the east coast, is by far the largest city on Hawaii with well over a third of the island's population. Kailua, on the west coast, is Hawaii's next largest community. Approximately 100 miles and two and a half to three hours driving time separate the two cities.

Visitors to Hawaii are able to drive around the circumference of the island. However, because of activity from **Mauna Loa** and **Kilauea**, the southern coastal roads have been frequently closed. Lava recently severed the coastal road at Kapapau and Highway 11 near the southwest corner of the island. Always check on the condition of the southern roads before starting off on a drive.

After exploring the west coast, visitors should also explore the other parts of the island, including the northern part of the island, the **Hamakua Coast**, **Hilo** and **Volcanoes National Park**. If you are going to drive the circumference of the island, plan to spend an entire day or spend the night in Hilo or at the **Volcano House** in Volcanoes National Park.

Honaunau Bay, the home of the Place of Refuge Park, offers some of the best snorkeling and shallow diving on the Island. The edges of the bay are rich in coral, fishes and other marine animals.

The Kona Coast

Most visitors to the Kona Coast land at the **Keahole Airport** just nine miles north of Kailua. The resort town of **Kailua** is the center of most activity on the Kona Coast and most of the dive charters on the Big Island launch from the **Kailua-Kona Harbor** or nearby **Honokohau Harbor**. There is a high concentration of hotels, restaurants and shopping malls mostly located around Alii Drive which heads south along the waterfront for about five miles from the wharf area. **Huggo's** is a good place for lunch or dinner, and it has a great view. The Sunday brunch at the **King Kamehameha** should not be missed. **Disappearing Sands Beach**, so named because its beautiful white sand periodically washes away and then reappears, is located several miles from town on Alii Drive. Stay along Alii Drive until it merges with the **Mamalahoa Highway** (11).

Continue on Route 11 south and turn right at the Kealakekua Bay sign, which is approximately 18 miles from Kailua. Stop at the coffee mill for a tour and a sample before heading into the town of **Napoopoo** situated at the water's edge. On the other side of the bay, a white monument has been erected where **Captain Cook** was killed in 1779. The cliffs above the monument are honeycombed with **Hawaiian Burial Caves**.

Located four miles further south on the southern tip of Honaunau Bay is the **Place of Refuge National Historical Park** which was a place of sanctuary for the early Hawaiians. This is also one of the best snorkeling spots in the islands.

There are two roads which head north out of Kailua. The Queen Kaahumanu Highway (19) follows the shoreline north to the Kohala Coast, past Honokohau Harbor and the Keahole Airport. At **Puako**, a small coastal town beyond the Mauna Lani Bay Hotel, are some of the finest examples of petroglyphs in the islands. North of Puako is **Hapuna Recreation Area**, displaying one of the island's most beautiful white sand beaches.

Further north, the Kohala Coast features fine luxury resorts which have a selection of excellent, although expensive, restaurants. At the northern tip of Kohala, in Hawi, there is the **Kohala Inn**, which serves very good oriental and American dishes at reasonable prices. The **Mauna Kea Beach Resort**, built more than 20 years ago, was one of the first world-class resorts in the islands. The recently opened **Hyatt Regency Waikoloa** spreads over 60 acres of oceanfront along the Kohala Coast.

At Waikui, Highway 19 turns east toward Waimea (also called Kamuela), a quiet cattle town and center of **Parker Ranch**, the largest individually owned ranch in the United States. Today there are approximately 50,000 cattle on the ranch. A second route to Waimea is the 39-mile drive from Kailua-Kona inland on Highway 190. If you get hungry in Waimea around dinner time, try the **Edelweiss Restaurant**.

A leaf scorpionfish blends with the coral and is often difficult to spot.

Kealakekua Bay is where Captain James Cook was killed by islanders in 1779. The Kona Aggressor live-aboard dive boat is moored near the monument erected in honor of Captain Cook.

Waimea To Hilo

From Waimea, Highway 19 heads east to the Hamakua Coast and then south along the coast to Hilo. At Honokaa, the first coastal community on the highway, the country becomes noticeably greener. The **Hawaiian Holiday Macadamia Nut Farm and Factory** in Honokaa offers tours and samples. For an interesting side trip from Honokaa go north on Highway 24 to the **Waipio Valley Lookout**. From the road's end, you can take an hour-and-a-half jeep tour to the black sand beach below. On the return through the valley, you will be rewarded with spectacular views of the 1,200 foot **Hiilawe Falls**.

Continue south on Highway 19. Turn off to Honomu on Route 220 to reach **Akaka Falls State Park**. A short nature trail leads past bamboo groves, ferns, ti and orchids to Akaka Falls, which plummets 420 feet down a sheer cliff face. Just to the south on Highway 19 is the turnoff for **Pepeekeo Scenic Drive** which winds 4 miles to the sea through jungled gulches on the old road into Hilo. Allow time to stop at the **Hawaii Tropical Botanical Gardens**.

The Tour To Kilauea

Kilauea, which has been erupting regularly since January of 1983, is one of the world's most active volcanoes. You must begin the tour in Hilo and drive south on Kanoelehua Highway 11. At Keaau, Volcano Road 11 turns to the right and rises across **Mauna Loa**'s lower slope toward the **Kilauea Crater** about 20 miles away. There is an admission charge to **Hawaii Volcanoes National Park** where visitors can see lava tubes, cinder cones, rain forest oases and ruins of stone temples. Numerous hiking trails cross the crater floors and meander beside the steaming vents. Brochures, maps and additional information are available at the Kilauea Visitor's Center which is open daily. Meals are served in **Volcano House** and the **Kilauea Lodge**.

The Kilauea crater is located at 4,000 feet, only part way up Mauna Loa's southern slope. The 11.1 mile long Crater Rim Road circles the wasteland of the Kilauea caldèra. Several marked trails honeycomb the area, including the well-known and well-named **Devastation Trail**.

From the center of the park, take the Chain of Craters Road 25 miles to the **Kalapana Coast**. This road dips back down to the sea past recently active small craters and barren lava flows. Kilauea's active vent is seven miles above the sea at Kupaianaha, but most of the lava flows underground emerging at the sea at **Upapau**. The eruption in December, 1986 covered the roads in **Kalapana**. Check with the Hawaiian Visitor's Bureau or the Visitor's Center at the park to find out which roads are currently open.

*Orange cup corals (*Tubastraea coccinea*) can be found underneath overhangs and on the ceilings of caves and archways. Each individual polyp sits in its own separate cup.*

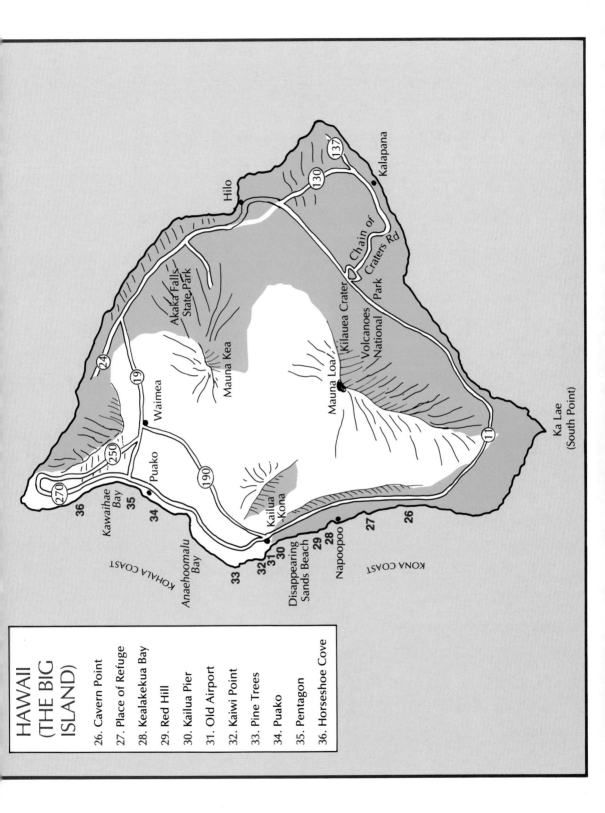

HAWAII (THE BIG ISLAND)

26. Cavern Point
27. Place of Refuge
28. Kealakekua Bay
29. Red Hill
30. Kailua Pier
31. Old Airport
32. Kaiwi Point
33. Pine Trees
34. Puako
35. Pentagon
36. Horseshoe Cove

DIVING THE BIG ISLAND

The diving on the Kona Coast is generally considered to be some of the best that the state of Hawaii has to offer. The waters off the Kona Coast are usually calm and clear year round. Ocean surface temperatures vary only by about 7 degrees from 73 in the winter to a high of 80 by late summer.

The island's high mountains provide protection from wind and rain and, because there is very little runoff, corals flourish and visibility is normally excellent—usually in the 100-foot range. In most places, the ocean floor drops off dramatically only a short distance from shore, providing excellent walls and an exciting mixture of deep-water pelagics and inshore reef animals. The underwater terrain, born of volcanoes, is honeycombed with lava tubes, arches, tunnels and caves.

KONA COAST

26. CAVERN POINT

DEPTH:	50 FEET
LEVEL:	INTERMEDIATE TO ADVANCED
ACCESS:	BOAT

Cavern Point is actually two dive sites, Twin Lava Tubes and Three Room Cave, which are located on the north side of Laeokamimi Point. This location offers the most extensive underwater lava tube system that has been discovered in the islands to date.

Devil scorpionfish are masters of disguise. Their grey to light brown coloring allows them to blend in well with rocky reefs and rubble bottoms. When swimming, however, their pectoral fins, which are banded in black, red, orange and yellow, are exposed, making them easy to spot.

At Twin Lava Tubes, there are two parallel underwater lava tubes, one on top of the other, that extend over 150 feet straight into the lava-rock wall. Massive cliffs tower above the water, plunging vertically to the ocean bottom 50 feet below the surface. A rock column, which rises out of the water, marks the entrance to the lava tubes. Immediately behind this rock pillar there is a spacious cavern. The two tubes are joined in the middle. The outer portion of the ceiling of the upper tube is partially out of the water.

Dive lights are necessary when exploring the interior of these tubes. Except for the light from the entrance, no light penetrates the depths of the tubes. The floors are a jumble of small boulders and rocks. There is very little sand or silt, so divers do not have to worry about stirring up sediment. However, because of the utter darkness, divers should always carry a backup light. When the ocean is rough, the outer cavern has a lot of surge.

The interior diameter of the tubes ranges from 10 to 20 feet. The walls are scored with cracks and crevices which hide a variety of cowries, shrimp and lobsters. Divers will also find bigeyes, glasseyes and schools of squirrelfishes. Nudibranchs are quite numerous, especially on the walls and floor of the cavern area.

At the Three Room Cave, there is an incredible complex of underwater caverns, with high vaulted ceilings and an endless number of caves and tunnels which lead off in all directions. Inside the caverns, divers will find Hawaiian lobsters, mole lobsters, slipper lobsters, spiny lobsters, cowries, shrimp, moray eels, turkeyfish and nudibranchs. The entrance to the caverns is on the north side of the point, at the base of a vertical wall at about 30 feet. There is an unconnected lava tube just north of the rear exit of the main complex and still more tubes on the south side of the point.

Twin Lava Tubes, one of the main attractions at Cavern Point, offers two parallel underwater lava tubes for exploration. The tubes measure between 10 to 20 feet in diameter. Here, a diver enters the lower tube.

Hawaiian lobsters are just one of many unusual residents of Three Room Cave at Cavern Point. This large area of interconnecting passageways and caverns also provides a home for other interesting invertebrates including cowries, shrimp and nudibranchs.

27. PLACE OF REFUGE

DEPTH:	25-130+ FEET
LEVEL:	NOVICE TO ADVANCED
ACCESS:	SHORE

Place of Refuge is perhaps the most protected of the shore diving along the Kona Coast and contains an amazing amount of tropicals.

Directions. Drive south on Route 11 out of Kailua-Kona, past the turnoff for Kealakekua Bay. Follow Route 160 approximately 20 miles south of Kailua until you pass mile marker 104. Turn right at the Pu'uhonua'O Honaunau (Place of Refuge at Honaunau) exit onto Keala-O-Keawe Street. Turn right just before the entrance to the parking area for the Place of Refuge National Historic Park. The best access is on the north side of the boat ramp. There are smooth lava steps which facilitate an easy entry into the water, but watch out for sea urchins.

The Dive. Swim straight out toward the point or to the right along the coastline. There are several parallel reefs topped with colorful corals in the middle of the bay in about 35 feet of water. Farther out, towards the mouth of the bay, a steep ledge drops quickly to 150 feet. One of the most interesting areas to explore is on the left side of the bay in the shallows, where finger ridges extend outward. The reef is full of holes that contain eels, crabs and shells. Turtles are also seen on virtually every dive. This site has incredible numbers of tropicals including yellow tangs, moorish idols and achilles tangs.

To the right of the entry point there is a shallow wall that hugs the coastline on the north side of the bay. There are many caves, arches and indentations in the wall. A flat shelf, which extends outward from the base of this wall, is covered with a variety of corals. Approximately 60 to 80 feet from the wall, this shelf drops off almost vertically to a flat sandy area which is over 100 feet deep. Eagle rays and manta rays are occasionally sighted here, as well as huge schools of tiny baitfish.

It is easiest to exit the water at the same place you entered, so you might want to mark the exact location with something visible from the water. There are picnic tables under the nearby Kiawe trees and restrooms at the park.

Caution. When heavy south swell is present, this site should be avoided.

The Place of Refuge, along the Kona Coast, is an excellent shore dive. Its protected waters are almost always calm and a large number of tropicals can be seen here. Natural steps in the lava shelf provide an easy entry.

28. KEALAKEKUA BAY

DEPTH:	15-100+ FEET
LEVEL:	NOVICE TO ADVANCED
ACCESS:	SHORE AND BOAT

This bay offers a variety of both shallow and deep diving. It was here that Captain Cook was killed.

Directions. Take Route 11 south from Kailua until you see the Kealakekua Bay sign, about 18 miles south of Kailua. Drive about 4 miles downhill past the coffee mill until you reach Napoopoo. Continue straight ahead until you reach the cement slab at water's edge.

The Dive. Access is easiest when the tide is high and the sea flat, as it usually is. Fishermen share this site and use the cement area for a loading platform. Because of the volume of small boat traffic, the use of a dive flag is recommended. Enter the water at the bottom of the steps and swim towards the mouth of the bay. The water is shallow, averaging between 15 and 30 feet, and the bottom is strewn with jagged lava formations and lots of coral. Schools of convict tangs, as well as yellow tangs, are often seen in this area. Other reef fishes that are common are surgeonfishes, ornate wrasse (Christmas wrasse) and parrotfishes.

Charter boats take snorkelers and divers to the north side of the bay near the Captain Cook monument which is not easily accessible from shore. Cook was killed here in a fight with local islanders in 1779. This large bay is teeming with tame fishes in part because they are fed every day by charter snorkeling operations.

Boat moorings have been placed in fairly shallow water on the inside of the bay where it is almost always calm. Clouds of colorful reef fishes, including rudderfishes, milletseed and raccoon butterflyfishes, durgeons, bird and saddle wrasses, and yellowtail coris swarm around divers and snorkelers as they enter the water. This section of the bay is often referred to as "The Aquarium." Divers will also find both color phases of forcepsfishes and longnose butterflyfish, large yellow margin eels and devil scorpionfish. Leaf scorpionfish are commonly seen in 10 to 15 feet of water around the monument.

The north side of the bay drops off into very deep water. The steep slope is overgrown with corals. The northern point of the bay can get quite surgy in the shallower areas.

The bright red spiral egg mass of a Spanish dancer is a common sight in the Red Hill area although these nudibranchs are rarely seen during the day.

A curious longjaw squirrelfish greets a diver in the cockpit of a plane sunk along the Kona Coast off Keahole Point.

29. RED HILL

DEPTH:	15-75 FEET
LEVEL:	INTERMEDIATE TO ADVANCED
ACCESS:	BOAT

Red Hill is located approximately 8 miles south of Kailua. The name comes from the red cliffs found between Keiki Waha Point and Keawakaheka Point, which are the result of red volcanic cinder cones which have become eroded. The area is actually a large bay which contains many popular dive sites. While some spots are suitable for novice divers, there are particular caves and deeper dives which require advanced skill levels.

The marine life is quite varied. The caves, lava tubes and tunnels host a variety of invertebrates, such as nudibranchs, Hawaiian lobsters, cowries and other cave dwellers. Divers frequently encounter small whitetip reef sharks nestled back in the farthest recesses of these caves. Hawaiian turkeyfish are fairly common. A dive light is a necessity for exploring the maze of lava formations. The entire Red Hill area can become quite surgy when there is a heavy swell.

Some of the most popular dive sites are the Amphitheater, the Dome, Long Lava Tube, Sharkies Cove and Driftwood Caverns. These areas are full of ridges, archways, skylights and tunnels, with good coral growth and lots of tropicals. Night dives at Red Hill are excellent and almost always produce such exotic creatures as Spanish dancers, Hawaiian lobsters and foraging conger eels.

30. KAILUA PIER

DEPTH:	10-30 FEET
LEVEL:	INTERMEDIATE
ACCESS:	SHORE

The Kailua Pier is a great spot for night dives and affords an easy entry and exit point. The pier itself has signs posted that diving is not allowed next to the pier. Enter the water inside the marina and swim out around to the right, offshore from the King Kamehameha Hotel.

The Dive. The shallow reef just outside the marina turns into a photographer's wonderland at night. Here, small puffers, boxfish, slipper lobster, nudibranchs, pencil urchins, shrimp and cowries dot the reefs. Divers will often encounter large conger eels out foraging for sleeping fishes.

31. OLD AIRPORT

DEPTH:	8-130+ FEET
LEVEL:	NOVICE TO ADVANCED
ACCESS:	SHORE

This old runway offers sites at both its north and south ends.

Directions. Locate the intersection of Kuakini and Palani in Kailua which is just above the King Kamehameha Hotel and the Kailua Wharf. Coming down Palani Road toward the wharf, turn right (north) on Kuakini and proceed to the old airport which is about a half-mile north of Kailua.

The entry at the north end of the runway is from a sandy beach at a small protected cove, which is only a short walk from the parking area. About 50 yards out, the bottom tapers to about 25 feet. Bear right and explore the wall packed with holes. This area has lots of red pencil urchin and small eels. Tropicals present include parrotfishes, surgeonfishes, tangs and wrasses. On the south side of the cove is an archway which is a good place to look for nudibranchs, flatworms and shells. Stay flat as you cross back over the shallow lava shelf because it is dotted with urchins.

The entry on the south end is much easier. Park on the ocean side of the south end of the runway where there is a sandy trail across the lave shelf to the water. You will find a small inlet cut into the lava on whose south edge are two flat shelves which provide steps. From these steps, you can do a giant stride into 8-foot deep water.

The small bay is ringed by underwater cliff walls which are full of crevices and overhangs. On the southern wall, there is a lava tube leading to a blowhole which can be explored on calm days. This location has a good variety of tropicals. The bottom drops rapidly, so watch the depth. The south end is a good night dive site because of the easy access and because it is partially lit by the lights of the adjacent ballfield and tennis courts. Dive this area first during the day and then return for a look at night. Expect to see varieties of lionfishes, puffers, octopuses, eels and shrimps, as well as an occasional Spanish dancer.

The Old Airport offers sites at both its north and south ends. This colorful yellow trumpetfish is only one of the many fishes that divers will see on every visit.

At night, divers at the Kailua Pier frequently encounter conger eels out foraging for food. This mustache conger has just caught a sleeping yellow tang, one of its favorite meals.

32. KAIWI POINT

DEPTH:	20-130+ FEET
LEVEL:	NOVICE TO ADVANCED
ACCESS:	BOAT

Kaiwi Point is located just to the north of Kailua. There is an excellent area to explore close to shore which averages only 20 to 25 feet. On the north side, there are a series of shallow coves extending inward along this shoreline. The walls of the coves are carved with recesses and caves hiding puffers, trumpetfishes and octopuses.

The area on the south side of the point offers a protected site which is usually very calm. Here, divers will find archways and large caves. There are usually a couple of whitetip reef sharks resting at the back of the cave directly behind the main arch. About 40 yards from shore, where the depth is 45 feet, the bottom plummets down a nearly vertical wall into very deep water. Hammerheads and manta rays are occasionally seen cruising this area.

This is a spectacular night dive site. The ceilings of the arch and the caves are covered with fields of bright orange tubastraea (cup corals). Lionfishes, slipper lobsters, Hawaiian lobsters and nudibranchs are all fairly common.

Red pencil urchins dot the reef along the Old Airport near Kailua.

Kaiwi Point, just to the north of Kailua, is an excellent area to explore close to shore. Friendly lemon butterflyfish often swarm around divers looking for a handout.

33. PINE TREES

DEPTH:	30-100+ FEET
LEVEL:	NOVICE TO INTERMEDIATE
ACCESS:	BOAT

This site is located several miles north of Kailua and is the most popular boat dive north of Kailua. It is actually a series of sites which offer a variety of terrain and marine life. There is a steep drop-off which runs parallel to shore as well as occasional strong currents in this area.

Carpenter's House. The bottom on the near-shore shelf averages 30 to 50 feet. The marine life includes blue-striped snapper, pyramid and banner butterflyfishes, eels, lionfishes, leaf scorpionfish, flame angels, tilefishes and dragon wrasse (juvenile rock movers).

Golden Arches. This is the site where divers will find "Miss Piggy," a well-known green sea turtle, who is almost always on hand to greet divers. The attractions at this site include large archways situated on the outside end of two ridges that extend seaward in 30 to 40 feet of water. There is a nearby drop-off that quickly falls below 100 feet. The ceilings of the archways are covered with an interesting assortment of invertebrates which include nudibranchs and cowries. This site also has a variety of rare animals, such as frogfishes, harlequin shrimps, dragon morays, black morays and lionfishes.

Pinnacle Peak. This site has some excellent shallow water diving, where there are lava tubes, arches and overhangs. The drop-off begins at about 50 feet. Here, divers will discover tame conger eels, whitemouth morays and yellow margin morays. The terrain has large pinnacles which are full of holes and caverns teeming with marine life. One or two frogfish can be found in this area on almost every dive.

Frogfishes are common at the Pine Trees. Because they are extremely territorial, dive guides are able to point them out on a regular basis.

The reef just outside of the marina and north of the Kailua Pier turns into a photographer's wonderland at night. Regal slipper lobsters are but one of the interesting invertebrates that can be seen emerging from their daytime hideaways.

Tiger cowries are called "leopard cowries" by the locals because of their spots. These are but one of the many shells commonly seen in Hawaii where the largest tiger cowries in the world are found.

The ornate butterflyfish is one of Hawaii's most beautiful reef fishes.

A steep drop-off can be found on the outside of the dive site at Red Hill. Manta rays and other large pelagics are often seen in blue water near this drop-off.

There are easy entry and exit points at Puako where visibility is usually excellent. When the ocean is calm, divers can swim over the lava shelf and dive a variety of interesting lava formations.

34. PUAKO

DEPTH:	10-100+ FEET
LEVEL:	INTERMEDIATE TO ADVANCED
ACCESS:	SHORE

This site consists of many finger ridges extending seaward. Visibility is almost always excellent.

Directions. Puako is located about 30 miles north of Kailua-Kona. To get there, take Route 19 north past the Keahole Airport and the Sheraton Royal Waikoloa Hotel. Look for the sign announcing Puako and turn left onto Puako Beach Road. Stay on the road past the boat ramp and drive through the residential area. At the end of the paved road, continue onto the solid sand road for about 25 yards and park.

The Dive. There is a fairly easy entry and exit area at the small cove. However, you should only dive here when it is calm. Swim over the shallow lava shelf watching carefully for spiny urchins. At about 50 to 75 yards offshore, turn to the right (north). You should be able to find three large vertical holes in the lava shelf which begin at a depth of about 10 feet and drop down to 25 feet. At the bottom, there is a short tunnel in which you may find squirrelfishes, trumpetfishes, devil scorpionfish and a variety of invertebrates. Exit the tunnel at a depth of about 30 feet on the ocean side.

Here finger ridges extend seaward. The channels between the ridges have sandy bottoms and are excellent spots to find the large, green sea turtles which frequent the area. The sandy areas also host a number of different shells including helmet shells, cone shells and augers. Leopard rays, which feed on the urchins, are fairly common. There is always an abundant variety of tropicals at this site and the visibility in the Puako reef area is usually excellent.

Caution. With the excellent visibility, it is easy to get into depths over 100 feet and on the outside part of the reefs, currents can be very strong.

35. PENTAGON

DEPTH:	20-35 FEET
LEVEL:	NOVICE
ACCESS:	BOAT

The Pentagon is located in the mouth of Anaehoomalu Bay on the Kohala Coast. This is a cavernous lava formation at the edge of a shelf in 20 to 35 feet of water. This site is so named because of the five massive openings which connect in a complex interweaving of countless smaller tunnels and archways. Because the area is so shallow, it is an excellent place for photography in and around the lava tubes.

This area has a wide variety of fishes including raccoon butterflyfishes, moorish idols, triggerfishes, tangs, surgeonfishes, and many others. The site is only 500 yards from the beautiful Waikoloa Beach.

The Pentagon, located in the mouth of Anaehoomalu Bay, consists of five massive openings which connect in a complex interweaving of tunnels and archways.

Divers will encounter giant porcupine pufferfish deep inside the lava tubes at Horseshoe Cove. These puffers often measure up to two feet in length and can inflate to the size of a basketball.

36. HORSESHOE COVE

DEPTH:	10-60+ FEET
LEVEL:	INTERMEDIATE TO ADVANCED
ACCESS:	BOAT

Horseshoe Cove is located north of Kawaihae Bay on the Kohala Coast. This site has a spectacular variety of lava tubes, caverns and tunnels. The anchorage is a mooring at the mouth of a large U-shaped cut which faces away from the shoreline. On the inside edge of the northern side of the horseshoe, there is a pronounced overhang in about 45 feet of water. A lava cave begins at this point. A tunnel leads off to the left from the rear of the cave, winding its way through the ridge for about 80 feet and exits on the outer side of the horseshoe.

North of this exit, there is a sloping ledge which is the underwater extension of a ridge that runs from the surface into the water.

Look for an entrance to a lava tube which begins at about 25 feet and runs parallel to the sloping ridge. The tube climbs gradually toward the surface. Many openings in the celling allow sunlight to filter into the tube. At the end, the tube surfaces inside a dome full of windows. Fresh water mixes with the saltwater, resulting in reduced visibility.

On the south side and inside edges of the horseshoe, there are myriad lava tubes which seem to stretch endlessly throughout the reef. The marine life here is abundant and almost every kind of tropical fish found in the islands will be seen in this area. In addition, there is a tremendous diversity of invertebrates including lobsters, nudibranchs, sea stars and urchins.

Caution. When the ocean is rough, it can become very surgy in the lava tubes. Be careful not to stir up silt because the disturbance can drastically reduce visibility, making it difficult to find your way out of the maze of lava tubes.

CHAPTER **VI** KAUAI

KAUAI AT A GLANCE

Kauai's heavy rainfall, many streams and extensive areas of verdant vegetation give much of the island the appearance of a South Seas paradise. Aptly called the "Garden Island," Kauai is the oldest of the major islands. Its 627 square miles were formed by a single shield volcano, Waialeale, which in over a million years of erosion has formed spectacular scenic landforms. Kauai's diverse terrain combines emerald cliffs, razor-sharp ridges, deep canyons, lush green valleys and beautiful white sand beaches.

Wawaikini, the island's highest peak, is one of the wettest places in the world, with an average rainfall of more than 400 inches per year. However, it is the dry Poipu Beach area on the southeastern coast that attracts most of the tourists. The tourist industry is also centered around Kapaa, on the east coast and, to a lesser extent, in Hanalei and Princeville on the north coast. The southeastern area is now a flat tableland covered with fields of sugarcane. Sugar and tourism are the island's principal industries but the island's farmers also grow macadamia nuts, taro, papayas and guavas. Most of Kauai's 40,000 inhabitants reside in the towns which line the shores, leaving the inland areas virtually uninhabited.

Haena Beach Park is one of many fabulous beaches on the north shore of Kauai. This protected beach is perfect for sunning and wading, even when the surf is rough.

Lumahai Beach, one of the most photographed beaches in the world, is located just west of Hanalei on Highway 56. This beautiful crescent-shaped beach epitomized the tropical paradise as "nurses' beach" in South Pacific *and is a wonderful place for a barefoot stroll.*

GETTING THERE

Kauai is located 95 miles northwest of Honolulu, barely a 20-minute flight into the main airport at Lihue. Aloha Airlines and Hawaiian Airlines provide inter-island connecting flights while United Airlines offers direct flights from Los Angeles and San Francisco. Several rental car companies maintain outlets at the airport and there is another smaller airport at Princeville which is serviced by Princeville Airways.

WHERE TO STAY

Kauai has a wide variety of accommodations which are located primarily in four areas: Poipu/Koloa (south shore), Lihue/Nawiliwili (east shore), Wailua/Waipouli/Kapaa (east shore) and Princeville/Hanalei (north shore). While most of the dive boat operations and popular boat dive sites are on the south shore, there are a few dive boat operations and a number of excellent shore dives which are located on the north shore. Therefore, all the areas are more or less convenient places to stay with respect to the proximity of the dive sites. On Kauai, it is more important to decide whether you want to be isolated from or a part of the crowds.

EXPLORING KAUAI

The pace on Kauai is a lot slower than on the other islands. There is one main road which runs around the perimeter of Kauai, from Ke'e Beach on the northern coast to Polihale Beach on the west coast. The road stops at each side of the rugged and impassable Na Pali Coast on the northwest side of Kauai. The roads are well maintained on Kauai and it is only a 40-mile drive from Lihue to the end of the road in either direction.

Ke'e Beach is located at the end of Highway 56. A hike along the Kalalau Trial, which rises quickly up along the steep Na Pali Cliffs, offers a magnificent view of the coastline.

North To Ke'e Beach

Set aside a full day for this trip, especially to include a 2-mile hike along the **Kalalau Trail**. A 10-minute drive north from Lihue on Kuhio Highway 56 is the **Wailua River**, the only navigable river in the state. From here tour boats leave from the Wailua Marina and travel three miles upriver to explore the famous **Fern Grotto**. After crossing the bridge spanning the river, turn left at the Coco Palms Resort onto Kuamoo Road (Highway 580) and drive two miles uphill into the valley to see the **Opaekaa Falls**. Continue on Highway 580 for scenic vistas of the upper Wailua River and, if time permits, visit **Smith's Tropical Paradise**, a 23-acre botanical garden.

Another ten minutes north on Highway 56 is the town of Waipouli, home of the **Coconut Plantation Market Place**, which offers a broad selection of restaurants, shops and boutiques, as well as hotels and condominiums. Between Waipouli and Kapaa, look inland for a profile of the sleeping giant formed by the mountain ridge. The quaint little hamlet of Kapaa is actually Kauai's most populated city.

This is a great place to break for lunch or dinner as there are some excellent restaurants in the area. The **Kintaro Restaurant** in Kapaa and the **Hanamaulu Cafe** in Hanamaulu both offer a first-rate sushi bar and other Japanese specialties. The **Bull Shed Restaurant** in Waipouli is a sure bet for a good steak.

The beginning of Kauai's north shore is marked by **Kilauea Point**. From there it is a short drive to the ranchlands and golf courses of **Princeville**, Kauai's largest resort community. After crossing the Kalihiwai River, the scenery becomes dominated by majestic mountains and dazzling ocean views. From Princeville to the end of Highway 56 are a series of valleys and beaches of incomparable beauty, beginning with the **Hanalei Valley** where over 50 percent of Hawaii's taro crop is cultivated. The bridge crossing the Hanalei River is the gateway to the small town of Hanalei. On Hanalei's main street are several companies which operate tours along the nearby **Na Pali Cliffs** using inflatable boats.

The Hanalei Valley Overlook is located near Princeville, Kauai's largest resort community. From this overlook, the Hanalei River can be seen winding its way through checkerboard fields of taro crop.

These two phyllidia nudibranchs are just a sample of the fascinating tiny animals found in Hawaiian waters.

A great place to stop for a fresh fish dinner is the **Hanalei Dolphin Restaurant**, located on Highway 56 where it crosses the river. Just down the road is Lumahai Beach, one of the most photographed beaches in the world.

Twin wooden bridges cross the river at Wainiha. Turn left after the second bridge and head up into the **Wainiha Valley** where you can stop at the **Wainiha Powerhouse** for a scenic view of the 4,000-foot high **Wainiha Pali Cliffs** and waterfalls. Highway 56 ends at **Ke'e Beach** where there is a beautiful, protected lagoon. From here, you can take the spectacular **Kalalau Trail** for a two-mile hike along the **Na Pali Cliffs** to **Hanakapiai Beach**. If you have worked up a good appetite, try **Charo**'s for lunch. It is located next to the Hanalei Colony Resort 2 miles from the end of the road.

Poipu Beach, on the sunny south shore, offers an array of facilities including restrooms and fresh water showers. This is an excellent site for snorkeling and swimming with its beautiful beaches and calm waters.

From Lihue to Polihale Beach

Leave early and plan to spend the entire day for a trip to **Waimea Canyon**. If you are staying on the east or north shore, arrange to stop for dinner in the Poipu area to avoid the rush hour traffic between Lihue and Wailua.

A side trip to **Nawiliwili**, a mile south of the capital city of Lihue, is a worthwhile excursion. Here, by the Huleia River banks at Nawiliwili, is where the opening scene from *Raiders of the Lost Ark* was filmed. Adjacent to this area is the **Menehune Fishpond**. To get there, take Rice Street to the town of Nawiliwili, then continue on Waapa Road to Hulemalu Road.

Next, head north on Hulemalu Road to Puhi Street and continue to the Kaumualii Highway (50). Turn left on Highway 50 and drive through the plantation town of Puhi. Turn south onto Highway 520 and continue through the naturally vaulted tunnel of eucalyptus trees to the town of Koloa. Turn right on Koloa Road and then left on Poipu Road. At the Poipu Beach sign on the rock wall, take the right fork to the end of Lawai Road and you will arrive at **Spouting Horn**, a well-known blow hole that resembles a geyser. **Koloa Landing**, which used to be the third largest port of the Hawaiian Islands after Honolulu and Lahaina, is located nearby. Today, Koloa Landing is often used as a dive training site.

Drive back down Lawai Road and turn right onto Poipu Road and you will come to popular **Poipu Beach** on your right. This is a very good snorkeling area with extensive facilities, including restrooms and fresh water showers. Poipu is the south shore's main resort area and one of Kauai's largest attractions with its sunny, dry weather, beautiful beaches and calm waters. A string of condominiums and hotels line the shore. Two recommended restaurants are **The Beach House** (expensive) and **Brenneke's Broiler** (moderate).

Highway 50 West proceeds through acre upon acre of sugarcane fields and a series of small towns, including Lawai and Hanapepe, along the southern coast. Lawai is the site of the 186-acre **Pacific Tropical Botanical Gardens** where the magnificent island flora can be observed. The older part of **Hanapepe** offers a fascinating assemblage of rickety wooden buildings and balconied Chinese shops reminiscent of the 19th century. **Waimea**, the town where Captain Cook first landed in the Hawaiian Islands, is replete with historical sites. As the sugarcane industry grew, Waimea was transformed into the bustling plantation town it is today.

Highway 50 ends 15 miles further at the southern tip of the Na Pali coast and there you will see the spectacular beach **Polihale State Park**. Both the Waimea Canyon Road and the better-maintained Kokee Road lead up to Waimea Canyon. These roads merge a few miles up the hill. **Waimea Canyon**, which is 3,500 feet deep, 2 miles wide and 10 miles long, is often referred to as the Grand Canyon of the Pacific. Two of the best lookout points to view the canyon's panoramas are Puu Ka Pele and Puu Hina Hina. The incredible **Kalalau Lookout** is located four miles beyond Kokee. At the end of the road, there is an easy trail from **Puu Kila Lookout**, affording panoramic views of the beautiful **Kalalau Valley**, which falls away 4,000 feet to the sea below.

A Yonge's gobi, measuring less than one-inch in length, rests on a stalk of whip coral along a ledge at Brenneke's Drop-off.

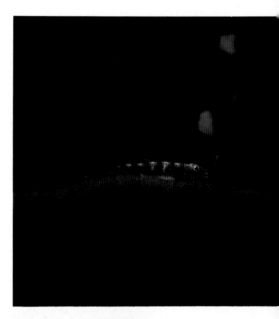

Koloa, which means "long cane," was the site of Hawaii's first sugarcane mill. Driving north on Highway 50 through Lawai, Kalaheo and Hanapepe, acres of sugarcane fields can be seen.

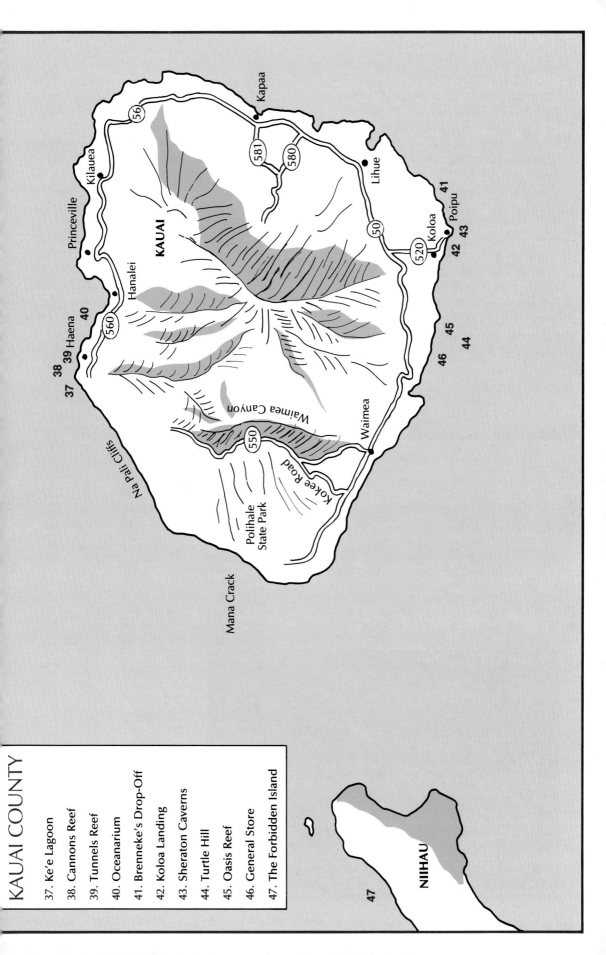

KAUAI COUNTY

37. Ke'e Lagoon
38. Cannons Reef
39. Tunnels Reef
40. Oceanarium
41. Brenneke's Drop-Off
42. Koloa Landing
43. Sheraton Caverns
44. Turtle Hill
45. Oasis Reef
46. General Store
47. The Forbidden Island

KAUAI

Kapaa

Kilauea

Princeville

Hanalei

Haena

Na Pali Cliffs

Waimea Canyon

Mana Crack

Polihale State Park

Kokee Road

Waimea

Lihue

Poipu

Koloa

NIIHAU

56
581
580
50
520
560
550

37
38
39
40
41
42
43
44
45
46
47

Diving Kauai

Most of the year-round diving is on the south shore, which offers an excellent selection of interesting boat dive locations. The north shore has some great shore dives, as well as remarkable boat dive sites. Because of the heavy surf during the winter months, the north shore is usually only diveable during the summer. The east side of the island is only accessible when the trade winds are calm, often during the winter.

In the summer when the winds diminish, there are opportunities for some exceptional and exciting advanced diving at the Mana Crack on the northwest shore of Kauai and off the nearby island of Niihau. Most of Kauai's dive shops and boat operations are located in the Wailua, Hanalei and Koloa/Poipu areas.

North Coast

37. KE'E LAGOON

DEPTH:	12-30 FEET
LEVEL:	NOVICE
ACCESS:	SHORE

Ke'e is a picturesque lagoon on the north side of Kauai that is often used for scuba training.

Directions. Drive north out of Lihue on Highway 56 and continue past Haena State Park to the end of the road.

The Dive. The inner lagoon is protected by a fringing reef. Swim along the natural channel formed between the reef and the shoreline and explore the many ledges. The lagoon is always calmer on the right side, but it is only 12 feet deep. The best diving inside the reef is on the left hand side, about 75 yards from the beach, where the bottom drops to a little over 20 feet. The coral in this area is lush and the terrain is a lot more interesting. There are schools of convict tangs, as well as many varieties of juveniles. Leaf scorpion fish are frequently seen in the shallows.

On the outside of the reef, there is a 30-foot drop-off which is full of caves and ledges to explore. However, this area is not accessible unless the ocean is flat because you have to cross over the top of the reef.

Ke'e Beach is an excellent spot for a family outing. The protected sandy beach is an absolutely beautiful setting for a picnic and the snorkeling is good. The highlight of this outing is a hike along the Kalalau Trail, which winds up along the Na Pali Cliffs.

Many Hawaiian reef fishes have a combination of unusual shapes and color patterns. This orange spine unicornfish, found at Cannons Reef, is an example with its bright orange lips and matching anal fin.

38. CANNONS REEF

DEPTH: 10-65 FEET

LEVEL: INTERMEDIATE TO
                   ADVANCED

ACCESS: SHORE

Also on the north shore, this site features a sandy beach entry and a drop-off.

Directions. The Cannons Reef is located 9.1 miles west of the entrance to Princeville and .35 miles past the Haena Dry Cave on the Kuhio Highway (56). There is an access trail to the right, just west of the Haena Beach Park before coming to a private driveway with a chain link fence. Pull off the side of the road and walk through the foliage down to the water.

The Dive. Just offshore from the sandy beach access, in 5 to 10 feet of water, there is a cut in the coral reef. Drop down at this point and swim through the cut to a wall that drops to 30 feet. Follow the wall to the left where the bottom drops fairly quickly to about 65 feet. Here, there is a large archway and many holes and caves in the wall. Tropicals, including surgeonfishes, moorish idols, parrotfishes and varieties of butterflyfishes are common. Occasionally you will encounter turtles and whitetip reef sharks. Be sure to mark your entry point so that you can exit the water at the same cut in the coral. The reef is usually diveable only during the summer months when the ocean is very calm.

Porcupine pufferfish are common to Oasis Reef on Kauai's south shore. When threatened, puffers will inflate themselves with water, hoping to discourage predators with their ominous look and "unswallowable" size.

Tunnels Reef is well-known for its lava tubes and caves. Bigeyed squirrelfish are often seen in the recesses of lava tubes.

39. TUNNELS REEF

DEPTH:	20-65 FEET
LEVEL:	NOVICE TO INTERMEDIATE
ACCESS:	SHORE

Tunnels Reef is also located on the north shore of Kauai, but on the east side of Haena Beach Park.

Directions. Drive north from Lihue on Highway 56 past Hanalei. At mile marker 36.6, turn right onto the dirt road which leads to the beach. Drive as far as you can and park your car. The access point is at the end of the dirt road.

The Dive. About 30 feet from shore there is a drop-off. Novice divers should follow the wall to the right, where they will find a patch of sandy bottom surrounded by reef. The shallow, inside reef is a good place for beginners to safely explore lava tubes.

Experienced divers can head out to the left of the boat channel where the sandy bottom slopes to about 65 feet. There are numerous ledges, caves and overhangs in the 50 and 60 foot range as well as lava tubes, interconnecting passageways and caverns.

Rudderfishes, parrotfishes, goatfishes and wrasses are usually present. There are also whitetip sharks and turtles in the area.

Caution. This site is normally only diveable in the summer. If the ocean is rough, access can be difficult with strong currents in deeper areas.

40. OCEANARIUM

DEPTH:	70-130+ FEET
LEVEL:	ADVANCED
ACCESS:	BOAT

41. BRENNEKE'S DROP-OFF

DEPTH:	50-90 FEET
LEVEL:	ADVANCED
ACCESS:	BOAT

The Oceanarium is a deep dive located on the north shore of Kauai. Here, three large pinnacles whose tops are 70 feet underwater, sit just seaward of a lava shelf. Swarms of fish congregate in the 120-foot deep channel between the shelf and the first pinnacle.

Black Coral. On the outside of the largest of the three pinnacles is a dramatic wall which plummets from 70 feet to 140 feet. The overhang at the top of this wall is covered with bright orange tubastraea and giant branches of black coral, measuring up to 8 feet in length. Large, hairy hermit crabs and rare boarfish are usually seen on the outside pinnacle.

This is also a good spot to photograph schools of blue-striped snapper, red goatfish and rarer fishes such as morwongs. Divers often see pelagics including rays, uluas and barracudas at the drop-off.

Brenneke's Drop-off, also called Brenneke's Ledge, is a lava shelf on the southeast shore of Kauai just east of Poipu. It extends for several miles parallel to shore and has a wall which drops to 90 feet. The underside of the many overhangs are covered with tubastraea and large branches of black coral. Long-nosed hawkfish hide amongst the coral. There are large schools of blue-striped snapper, and also resident whitetip sharks and turtles. In the caves and ledges at the base of the drop-off, divers will discover cowries, lobsters and moray eels. On top of the plateau at about 50 feet, there are lots of coral, octopuses and tropicals.

Caution. There are often strong currents here. Do not dive when the ocean is rough.

Large, hairy hermit crabs, such as this specimen which measures 8 inches across and makes it home in a triton's trumpet shell, can regularly be seen at the Oceanarium, a dive site on the north shore of Kauai.

42. KOLOA LANDING

DEPTH:	30-50 FEET
LEVEL:	NOVICE TO INTERMEDIATE
ACCESS:	SHORE

Koloa Landing, on the southeast shore, west of Poipu, is a popular shore dive often used for training dives. A launching ramp provides easy entries and exits and the area is almost always calm. It is also a popular night dive location.

Directions. Drive south from Lihue on Highway 50. Turn left onto Route 250 towards Koloa. Turn right onto Koloa Road at the stop sign and then left onto Poipu Road. At the large Poipu Beach sign, take the right fork which becomes Lawai Road and head toward Spouting Horn. Then take the first left onto Hoonai Road. About a quarter of a mile further, you will come upon a broken asphalt road which leads down to Koloa Landing.

The Dive. Enter the water using the ramp and swim to the left out along the live coral reef. About a quarter-mile from shore, this reef drops down to 50 feet where large schools of tame fishes and lots of crustaceans and invertebrates can be found. To the right, there are nice coral formations on a white sand bottom in about 30 feet of water. This area is well-protected year round and often has excellent visibility.

43. SHERATON CAVERNS

DEPTH:	30-60 FEET
LEVEL:	NOVICE TO INTERMEDIATE
ACCESS:	BOAT

The Sheraton Caverns, also known as "The Circus," is located on the south shore of Kauai, just west of Poipu.

Dive boats usually anchor in about 60 feet of water on the sand bottom. Recently divers have been greeted at the dive platform by Pepe and LaPue, two very friendly green sea turtles which inhabit the area. These turtles often hang around the boat for the whole dive and make excellent photographic subjects.

Brenneke's Drop-off (also known as Brenneke's Ledge) is a lava shelf which extends along several miles of Kauai's southeastern shore.

Koloa Landing, on Kauai's southeastern shore, makes an excellent night shore dive. This sheltered site often has excellent visibility and provides a haven for unique fishes such as this white-spotted toby.

Lava Tubes. The main attractions of the site, however, are the tubes, archways, tunnels and ledges. Especially well-known are the three, large diameter, parallel lava tubes which make this the most popular cavern dive on Kauai.

Another highlight of this site is the number of large whitemouth morays, conger eels and other eel varieties that will emerge from the reef and swim with divers. The marine life also includes all kinds of tropicals, schools of blue-striped snappers (ta'ape), spiny and slipper lobsters, shrimps, cowries and lionfishes.

44. TURTLE HILL

DEPTH:	40-90+ FEET
LEVEL:	NOVICE TO ADVANCED
ACCESS:	BOAT

Turtle Hill, also called Turtle Bluffs, is located on the south shore near Oasis Reef and the General Store, just on the ocean side of the red marker buoy number 2. This area consists of plateaus 40 to 50 feet deep interspersed with pinnacles which protrude from a sandy, rubble bottom over 90 feet deep.

Green Sea Turtles. The site is named for one of these plateaus which is frequented by a large number of green sea turtles, as well as octopuses and whitetip reef sharks. This plateau is on the north side of a crescent-shaped cut in the large, flat lava shelf which extends from shore.

There are lots of caves, ledges, arches and overhangs to explore which are inhabited by lobsters, menpachi and a variety of invertebrates. Schools of blue-striped snappers, durgeons, pyramid butterflyfish and pennantfish are usually encountered. A few of the rare boarfish are frequently seen near the base of a small pinnalce at the north edge of the crescent-shaped cut.

45. OASIS REEF

DEPTH:	35 FEET
LEVEL:	NOVICE
ACCESS:	BOAT

Oasis Reef rises from a flat, sandy bottom in 35 feet of water, just west of Kukuiula on the southeast coast. The reef is roughly 100 feet by 40 feet and includes a lone pinnacle which rises to within a few feet of the surface.

Pennantfish. Divers will find large schools of pennantfish which are false moorish idols. There are literally thousands of tropicals in this area, including triggerfishes, butterflyfishes and porcupine puffers. The reef is full of holes and cracks where divers will find banded coral shrimps, lobsters, hermit crabs, octopuses, moray eels and lots of nudibranchs. This is also a good place to hunt for shells.

46. GENERAL STORE

DEPTH:	60-90 FEET
LEVEL:	INTERMEDIATE TO ADVANCED
ACCESS:	BOAT

This area is located on the south shore, west of Kukuiula. It is named the General Store because a little bit of everything can be found here. Actually, it is a U-shaped rock formation approximately 60 feet deep on top and 90 feet at the bottom. Littered about the bottom are the remains of an 1800's steamship including several large anchors, boilers and pieces of chain.

There are three main lava tubes here and several caverns full of marine life. At about 70 feet, black coral trees line the ceiling of the caverns where divers will find long-nosed hawkfish. There are also large schools of lemon butterflyfish which will follow divers, looking for a handout. Manta rays, hammerheads and turtles are frequently spotted as well.

NIIHAU

47. THE FORBIDDEN ISLAND

DEPTH:	TO 130+ FEET
LEVEL:	ADVANCED
ACCESS:	BOAT

Niihau is a private island off the northwest side of Kauai. The three-hour boat trip to this site is well worthwhile because of the near-virgin diving, incredible underwater canyons and drop-offs. Encounters with large pelagics such as this beautiful oceanic whitetip shark are common.

Niihau is located 17 miles west of Kauai across the Kaulakahi Channel. Until recently, it was forbidden for outsiders to set foot on this island. In 1987, the Niihau Ranch instituted limited helicopter service to the island, offering visits to two remote beaches. It is 70 square miles in size, making it the 7th largest island. To this day, Niihau has remained a cultural preserve, maintaining the traditions, culture and language of old Hawaii.

Today, Bubbles Below and Aquatics Kauai run dive trips to Niihau on an infrequent basis during the summer months. Because the trip takes approximately 3 hours by boat, excursions depend upon ocean conditions and weather. The coastal areas offer near-virgin diving. Although there is not a substantial amount of coral, the underwater sites feature incredible drop-offs, underwater canyons, giant sea arches and cathedrals, and an abundance of large marine life. Rays, sharks, jacks, tuna, ulua and other gamefish are frequently encountered.

CHAPTER VII   HAWAII'S MARINE LIFE

Hawaii's warm, blue waters are well-known for the variety of beautiful and colorful reef fishes which they harbor. Divers will commonly see moorish idols, endless varieties of butterflyfishes, trumpetfishes, wrasses and squirrelfishes. In some areas, the fish are accustomed to being fed and will literally swarm divers as they enter the water. In addition to these clouds of friendly fishes, there are many unique species found only in Hawaiian waters. There are also a few potentially harmful creatures, although they are not normally aggressive. As a general rule, you should not touch or handle anything which is unfamiliar.

If you wish to locate a particular type of fish to observe or photograph, the local dive shops can help. Because most marine animals are territorial, dive guides can usually take you to a site frequented by your quarry.

The Hawaiian Islands play host to more than 400 species of reef and inshore fishes, approximately 30 percent of which are believed to be unique to the area. Among the more colorful of these common reef fishes are milletseed, raccoon and pyramid butterflyfishes, saddleback wrasse, parrotfishes, surgeonfishes, trumpetfishes, forcepsfishes, pennantfish, blue-striped snappers and yellow tangs.

Moorish Idol (Zanclus cornutus Linnaeus).

Forcepsfish (Forcipiger flavissimus).

UNUSUAL MARINE LIFE

Frogfish

The frogfish, also called an anglerfish, is one of the most fascinating creatures in Hawaiian waters. They are best known for their unique method of attracting prey by using their long first dorsal spine as a lure which they dangle in front of their mouth. Almost all frogfishes are sedentary, spending most of their lives sitting motionless on the bottom. This ungainly and rather homely fish has an uncanny ability to blend in with various backgrounds, disguising itself as different forms of substrate including algae-encrusted rocks, sponges, tunicates and sea grasses.

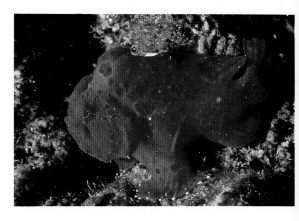

Frogfish (Antennariidae).

Green Sea Turtles

Encounters with green sea turtles in Hawaii are becoming increasingly common. Most of these turtles average 40 inches in length, but can grow to five feet. Their shells are mottled brown and olive green. Their name is actually derived from the color of their body fat. Green turtles can be distinguished by the single pair of scales on the front of their head. As adults, they frequent shallow coastal waters, especially in rocky areas and coral reefs.

Green Sea Turtle (Chelonia mydas).

Harlequin Shrimp

The harlequin shrimp (*Hymenocera picta*) is aptly named for its gaudy appearance. It averages 1 to 1-1/2 inches in length and can often be found deep inside the crevices of large coral heads. This shrimp is becoming relatively scarce, in part because it is highly prized by aquarists. Sea stars constitute one of its favorite foods.

Harlequin Shrimp (Hymenocera picta).

Humpback Whale (Megaptera novaeangliae).

Humpback Whales

Humpback whales can be found in Hawaiian waters from November through May, although the best time to see them is from January through early April when they congregate in the greatest numbers between the islands of Maui, Kahoolawe, Lanai and Molokai. It is believed that between 400 and 500 humpback whales make an annual migration to Hawaii each year to breed. Adult humpback whales can measure up to 50 feet in length.

Although few divers are lucky enough to actually see these whales underwater, almost everyone who dives in Hawaii during the humpback breeding season will clearly hear their songs.

Manta Rays

The gentle giant of Hawaiian waters is easily recognizable by the two large flaps beneath its head which are used to funnel plankton into its mouth. This graceful animal has a wingspan that can exceed 20 feet. It is harmless to man, lacking a barb or stinger on its tail. Manta rays are frequently seen cruising near the surface along drop-offs.

Manta Ray (Manta alfredi).

Spanish Dancer Nudibranchs

The largest of the vast array of colorful nudibranchs found in Hawaiian waters is the Spanish dancer (*Hexabranchus sanguineus*) which may reach 10 inches in length. Discovering a red Spanish dancer foraging on the brilliant white sand at night can be quite startling since most divers are accustomed to seeing nudibranchs less than 2 inches in length. As it feeds, it creeps slowly along on its soft, yet firm muscle that resembles the sole of a shoe.

Velvety to the touch, the Spanish dancer's gills are clustered on its back, giving the appearance of a bouquet of flowers. This nudibranch is especially spectacular when it moves from the sand to swim in open water.

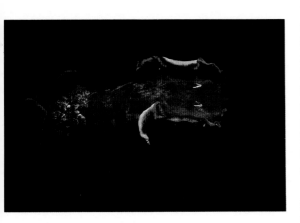

Spanish Dancer Nudibranch (Hexabranchus sanguineus).

POTENTIALLY DANGEROUS MARINE LIFE

Cone Shells

Cone shells are carnivorous predators that subdue their prey by shooting them with a venomous harpoon. The harpoon is released from the snout, located at the narrow end of the shell. Because their venom can be harmful to humans, they should be handled only from the broad end and always with caution. Most of the cone shells found in Hawaiian waters measure from ¾ of an inch to 3 inches in length.

Textile Cone Shell (Conus textile).

Crown-of-Thorns

The crown-of-thorns sea star (*Acanthaster planci*) feeds voraciously on living corals. The characteristic large, sharp spines which grow on its back can cause a painful wound and should be avoided. The sea star averages 12 inches in diameter and is reddish-orange in color.

Crown-of-Thorns Sea Star (Acanthaster planci).

Eels

Eels can be found almost anywhere there are cracks and crevices in which to hide. They are normally not aggressive unless threatened. Feeding and handling eels should be left to the dive tour leaders.

There are a number of very colorful and interesting eels in Hawaii. Most moray eels can be seen during the day and some reach lengths of over 6 feet. Conger eels are nocturnal predators and can often be seen prowling the reefs looking for sleeping fishes.

Whitemouth Moray Eel (Gymnothorax meleagris).

*Hawaiian Turkeyfish (*Pterois sphex*).*

Hawaiian Turkeyfish

Due to the toxicity of the poison contained in its spines, the Hawaiian turkeyfish (*Pterois sphex*) is considered dangerous even though it is slow moving. Divers must use extreme caution photographing or examining it at close range. An adult can reach 9 inches in length with spines extending well beyond the connecting membranes. Reddish-brown in color and marked with vertical lines, the turkeyfish can frequently be found swimming upside-down along the ceilings of caves or lava tubes.

*Whitetip reef sharks (*Triaenodon obesus*).*

Sharks

The most common type of shark seen in Hawaiian waters is the whitetip reef shark, a relatively sluggish bottom dweller often found foraging over the reef floor or resting in caves and lava tubes. Whitetips may return to the same cave and are generally considered to be harmless, but divers should be careful not to corner them or provoke them in any way.

Few divers are lucky enough to actually see other types of sharks near shore. Occasional sightings are made of hammerheads, gray reef sharks, galapagos sharks, blacktip sharks and oceanic whitetip sharks.

*Spiny Urchin (*Echinothrix sp.*).*

Spiny Sea Urchins

Urchins are especially common in shallow areas, but are also found at depth. At night, urchins will come out of their hiding place to forage. The venomous variety of spiny sea urchins have long, slim, needle-like spines which may be all white, or black, or with white and black bands. All these urchins have two types of spines, long hollow ones and shorter, venom-tipped ones. The spines can penetrate wetsuit material and even the slightest contact with the brittle spines can cause them to break off and become embedded in the skin. Embedded bits of spine can be very painful and serious punctures may require medical attention.

Scorpionfishes and Lionfishes

Hawaii has more than two dozen species of scorpionfishes and lionfishes. These bottom-dwelling rockfishes have the ability to inject poison through spines in their dorsal, anal and pelvic fins. These fishes are carnivorous and believed to be nocturnal. While they are found prowling the reefs and sandy bottoms at night, most of their time is spent motionless. Even though these fishes are slow moving, divers should be very careful not to touch them because their sting can be quite serious.

Barber's Scorpionfish

Another rare scorpionfish is the Barber's (*Dendrochirus barberi*) which is usually found in the open at night around rocky recesses or on rubble and sandy bottoms where the water is calm. The color of this fish is reddish-brown or greenish-brown, and it has irregular, wide, vertical markings or stripes. It can grow up to 6 inches and can easily be recognized by its rounded, oversized pectoral fins.

Barber's Scorpionfish (Dendrochirus barberi).

Devil Scorpionfish

This scorpionfish (*Scorpaenopsis diabolus*) is grey to light brown, which enables it to blend well with the rocky reefs and rubble bottom. The only time that this fish is easy to spot is when it swims, exposing its pectoral fins which are banded in black, red, orange and yellow. Its small eyes are located high in the head. Large specimens may grow to 12 inches.

Devil Scorpionfish (Scorpaenopsis diabolus).

*Leaf Scorpionfish (*Taenianotus triacanthus*).*

Leaf Scorpionfish

The three-spined or leaf scorpionfish (*Taenianotus tricanthus*) is among the smallest of the scorpionfishes, averaging 2 to 3 inches in length. The fins of this rare little fish give it an irregular leaf-like appearance, hence its common name. The fish has a distinct yellow, black and red color phase and is very territorial, often seen in the identical spot from year to year.

*Titan Scorpionfish (*Scorpaenopsis cacopsis*).*

Titan Scorpionfish

The body of this species (*Scorpaenopis cacopsis*) is more elongated than the devil scorpionfish. Its color pattern is mottled and uneven, usually reddish brown with white and yellow. Its head is more angular and its eyes are set much higher than the end of its snout. Large specimens will reach 20 inches in length. It is normally found on the outer edge of the reef, at depths below 20 feet.

APPENDIX 1

EMERGENCY NUMBERS

Kauai, Oahu and Maui

	911 or "0" for operator
Hawaii	**961-6022 or "0" for operator**
Coast Guard	**(800) 331-6176**
Diver's Alert Network	**(919) 684-8111**

HYPERBARIC CHAMBERS

Hyperbaric Treatment Center   **523-9155**
42 Ahui St.
Honolulu, Oahu

Kauai Veterans Memorial Hospital **338-9431**
4643 Waimea Canyon Dr.
Waimea, Kauai

Maui Memorial Hospital   **242-2343**
(one man chamber)
221 Mahalani St.
Wailuku, Maui

HOSPITALS

Hawaii

Hilo Hospital   **969-4111**
1190 Waianuenue Ave.

Kona Hospital   **322-9311**
Kealakekua Town

Kaui

Wilcox Memorial Hospital   **245-1100**
3420 Kuhio Highway, Lihui

Maui

Kaiser Permanente Medical Care

  Lahaina Clinic   **661-0081**
  910 Wainee

  Wailuku Clinic   **242-7311**
  80 Mahalani

Oahu

Queen's Medical Center   **538-9011**
1301 Punchbowl, Honolulu

When contacting an emergency number be sure to state your name, exact location and the nature of the emergency. Stay on the phone until the operator confirms that all the information has been received correctly. Stay on the scene to give the responding unit additional information and assistance.

DAN

The Divers Alert Network (DAN) operates a 24-hour emergency number **(919) 684-8111** (collect calls accepted if necessary) to provide divers and physicians with medical advice on treating diving injuries. DAN also maintains up-to-date information on the locations of recompression chambers accepting sport divers. In addition, they can organize air evacuation to the nearest recompression chamber.

Since many emergency room physicians do not know how to properly treat diving injuries, it is highly recommended that in the event of an accident, you have the physician consult a DAN doctor specializing in diving medicine.

DAN is a publicly supported, not-for-profit membership organization. Membership is $15 a year and includes a first aid manual and the newsletter *Alert Diver* which discusses diving medicine and safety. DAN members are also able to buy a $25 medical insurance policy which covers hospitalization, air ambulance and recompression chamber treatment for diving injuries. Divers should check with their insurance companies since many policies do not cover specialized treatment for diving accidents.

DAN's address is: Divers Alert Network, Box 3823, Duke University Medical Center, Durham, NC 27710. Their non-emergency number is (919) 684-2948.

APPENDIX 2

SCUBA DIVING CENTERS & DIVE CHARTERS

Oahu

Aaron's Dive Shop, Inc.
1. 602 Kailua Rd.
  Kailua, HI 96734
  (808) 262-2333
2. 46-216 Kahuhipa St.
  Kaneohe, HI 96744
  (808) 395-5922

Alii Divers
1356 B Kaiolani Blvd.
Honolulu, HI 96814
(808) 944-9762

Aloha Dive Shop
Koko Marina Shopping Center
Hawaii-Kai
Honolulu, HI 96825
(808) 395-5922

Aqua Blue Adventures
Ward Center
1050 Ala Moana Blvd.
Honolulu, HI 96814
(808) 521-9072

Aqua Marine
1313 9th Ave.
Honolulu, HI 96816
(808) 732-7374

Atlantis Reef Divers
(Dive Team Hawaii Group)
1085 Ala Moana Blvd. #102
Honolulu, HI 96814
(808) 522-5801
(800) 554-6267

Bojac Aquatic Center
94-801 Farrington Hwy.
Waipahu, HI 96797
(808) 671-0311

Breeze Hawaii Diving Adventures Corp.
3014 Kaimuki Ave.
Honolulu, HI 96826
(808) 955-4541

Dan's Dive Shop
660 Ala Moana Blvd.
Honolulu, HI 96813
(808) 536-6181
(800) 527-6377

Divestar of Hawaii
94-1139 Polinahe Pl.
Waipahu, HI 96797
(808) 677-7337

Down Under Divers
94-866 Moloalo, Bldg. B-13
Waipahu, HI 96797
(808) 671-1065

Elite Dives Hawaii
67-239 B Kahaone Loop
Waialua, HI 96791
(808) 637-9331

First Dive Tours, Inc.
2301-A Waiomao Rd.
Honolulu, HI 96816
(808) 732-6972

Hawaii Sea Adventures
98-718 Moanaloa Rd.
Pearl City, HI 96782
(808) 487-7515

Leeward Dive Center
87-066 Farrington Hwy.
Maili, HI 96792
(808) 696-3414
(800) 255-1574

Oahu School of Diving and Pro Dive
95 S. Kamehameha Hwy.
Wahaiwa, HI 96786
(808) 622-2283

Ocean Adventures, Inc.
98-406 Kamehameha Hwy.
Pearl City, HI 96782
(808) 487-9060
(800) 387-8047

Ocean Motion Divers
% Turtle Bay Hilton
Hahuku, HI 96731
(808) 293-8811 Ext. 6597

Rainbow Divers
1640 Wilikina Dr.
Wahaiwa, HI 96786
(808) 622-4532

South Pacific Scuba
740 Kapahulu Ave.
Honolulu, HI 96816
(808) 735-7196

South Seas Aquatics
(800) 252-6244
1. 870 Kapahulu Ave. #202
    Honolulu, HI 96816
    (808) 735-0437
2. Ana Kalakaua Center
    2155 Kalakaua Ave. Suite 112
    Waikiki Beach, HI 96815
    (808) 922-0852

Surf & Sea
62-595 Kam. Highway
Haleiwa, HI 96712
(808) 637-9887

Waikiki Diving Center
1734 Kalakaua Ave.
Honolulu, HI 96826
(808) 955-5151

Vehon Diving Ventures
Hawaii-Kai Shopping Center
377 Keahole St.
Honolulu, HI 96825
(808) 396-9738

Maui

Aquatic Charters of Maui
132 Kapuna St.
Kihei, HI 96753

Beach Activities of Maui
% Sheraton Maui
P.O. Box 10056
Lahaina, HI 96761
(808) 661-0031

Bill's Scuba Shack
36 Keala Place
Kihei, HI 96753
(808) 879-3483
(800) 950-3483

Capt. Nemo's Ocean Emporium
150 Dickenson St.
Lahaina, HI 96761
(808) 661-5555

Destination Pacific Charters
140 Uwapo Rd., Suite 3-201
Kihei, HI 96753
(808) 874-0305
(800) 657-7769

Dive Maui, Inc.
Lahaina Market Place
Lahainaluna Rd.
Lahaina, HI 96761
(808) 667-2080

The Dive Shop of Kihei, Ltd.
P.O. Box 917
1975 S. Kihei Rd.
Kihei, HI 96753
(808) 879-5172
(800) 367-8047 Ext. 368

Ed Robinson's Diving Adventures
P.O. Box 616
Kihei, HI 96753
(808) 879-3584
(800) 635-1273

Extended Horizons
P.O. Box 10785
Lahaina, HI 96761
(808) 667-0611

Finisterre Diving Services
Suite 117, PCB
Kahului, HI 96732
808-874-5529

Hawaiian Reef Divers
129 Lahainaluna Rd.
Lahaina, HI 96761
(808) 667-7647

Lahaina Divers
(Dive Team Hawaii Group)
(800) 657-7885
1. 710 Front St.
    Lahaina, HI 96761
    (808) 667-7496
2. Whalers Village
    Kaanapali, HI 96761
    (808) 667-4077

Makena Coast Charters
P.O. Box 1599
Kihei, HI 96753
(808) 874-1273

Maui Dive Shop
1. 279 Wahea Ave.
    Kahului, HI 96732
    (808) 871-2111
2. Kihei Town Center
    Kihei
    (808) 879-1919
3. Azeka Place
    Kihei
    (808) 879-3388
4. Kamaole Shopping Center
    Kihei
    (808) 879-1533
5. Lahaina Cannery
    Lahaina
    (808) 661-5388

6. Wailea Shopping Village
    Wailea
    (808) 879-3166
7. Kahana Gateway
    Lahaina
    (808) 669-3800

Maui Sun Divers
P.O. Box 565
Kihei, HI 96753
(808) 879-3631

Mike Severns Scuba Diving
P.O. Box 627
Kihei, HI 96753
(808) 879-6596

Molokini Divers
1993 S. Kihei Rd., Bay 22
Kihei, HI 96753
(808) 879-0055

Ocean Activities Center
3750 Wailea Alanui D-2
Kahaina, HI 96761
(808) 879-7427
(800) 367-8047 Ext. 448

Ocean Enterprises
P.O. Box 1463
Kihei, HI 96753

Scuba Schools of Maui, Inc.
1000 Limahana Place
Lahaina, HI 96761
(808) 661-8036

Sundance Scuba Charters
1975 S Kihei Rd.
Lahaina, HI 96761
(808) 667-2842

Underwater Habitat, Inc.
P.O. Box 1087
Kihei, HI 96753
(808) 244-9739

Hawaii

AAA Dive Kona
P.O. Box 1780
Kailua-Kona, HI 96745
(800) 562-3483

Aggressor Fleet
Kona Aggressor
P.O. Drawer K
Morgan City, LA 70381
(800) 348-2628

Aquatic Adventures
P.O. Box 160
Moon's Center
Kamuela, HI 96743
(808) 885-6303

Big Island Divers
74-425 Kealakehe Pkwy. #7
Kailua-Kona, HI 96740
(808) 329-6068

Captain Ken's Kona
P.O. Box 4308
Kailua-Kona, HI 96745
(808) 328-8695

Dive Makai Charters
P.O. Box 2955
74-5590 Alapa St.
Kailua-Kona, HI 96745
(808) 329-2025

Echo.Scapes
75-5626 Kuakini Hwy.
King Kamehameha Sq.
Kailua-Kona, HI 96740
(808) 329-7116

Fair Wind
78-7128 Kaleopapa Rd.
Keauhou Bay
Kona, HI 96740
(808) 322-2788

Fantasy Divers
73-4125 Hawaii Belt Rd.
Kailua-Kona, HI 96740

Free Divin' Hawaii
P.O. Box 5341
Kailua-Kona, HI 96745
(808) 329-5228

Jack's Diving Locker
Coconut Grove Market Place
75-5819 Alii Dr.
Kailua-Kona, HI 96745
(808) 329-7585
(800) 345-4807

King Kamehameha Divers
75-5660 Palani Rd.
Kailua-Kona, HI 96740
(808) 525-7234
(800) 329-5662

Kohala Divers
Kawaihae Shopping Center
P.O. Box 4935
Kawaihae, HI 96743
(808) 882-7774

Kona Aggressor
(Live-Dive Hawaii, Inc.)
P.O. Box 2097
Kailua-Kona, HI 96745
(808) 329-8182
(800) 344-5662

Kona Coast Divers
(Dive Team Hawaii Group)
75-5614 Palani Rd.
Kailua-Kona, HI 96740
(808) 329-8802
(800) 562-3483

Kona Kai Diving
P.O. Box 4178
Kailua-Kona, HI 96745
(808) 329-0695

Mauna Lani Sea Adventures
Mauna Lani Hotel
P.O. Box 4000
Kawaihae, HI 96743
(808) 885-7883

Nautilus Dive Center
382 Kamehama Ave.
Hilo, HI 96720
(808) 935-6939

Ocean Sports Waikoloa
P.O. Box 5000
Kohala Coast, HI 96743
(808) 885-5555

Red Sail Sports
One Waikoloa Beach Dr.
Waikoloa, HI 96743
(800) 255-6425

Sandwich Isle Divers
75-5729 I Alii Dr.
Kailua-Kona, HI 96740
(808) 329-9188

Scuba Schools of Kona
74-425 Kaelakehe Pkwy.
Kailua-Kona, HI 96740

Sea Dreams Hawaii
77-6470 Leilani St.
Kailua-Kona, HI 96740
(808) 329-8744
(800) 366-3483

A Sea Paradise, Scuba
78-7128 Kaleopapa Rd.
Kailua-Kona, HI 96745
(808) 322-2500
(800) 322-5662

Sun Seeker
P.O. Box 2442
Kailua-Kona, HI 96745
(808) 322-6774

Trident Dive
P.O. Box 3513
Kailua-Kona, HI 96740

Kauai

Aquatics Kauai
(Dive Team Hawaii Group)
733 Kuhio Hwy.
Kapaa, HI 96746
(808) 822-9213
(800) 822-9422

Beach Activities of Kauai
Sheraton Princeville Hotel
P.O. Box 3250
Princeville, HI 96722
(808) 826-6851

Bubbles Below
6251 Hauaala Rd.
Kapaa, HI 96746
(808) 822-3483

Dive Kauai
4-976 Kuhio Hwy. Suite 4
Kapaa, HI 96746
(808) 822-0452
(800) 828-3483

Fathom Five Divers
P.O. Box 907
Koloa, HI 96756
(808) 742-6991

Get Wet Kauai
4442 Makaha Rd.
Kapaa, HI 96746
(808) 822-4884

Kauai Divers
RR-1
P.O. Box 56
Koloa, HI 96756
(808) 742-1580

Kauai Sea Sports, Inc.
2827 Poipu Rd.
Koloa, HI 96756
(808) 742-6570

Ocean Odyssey
Located at Kauai Hilton & Beach Village
P.O. Box 807
Kapaa, HI 96746
(808) 822-9680

The Poipu Dive Company
Kiahuna Shopping Village
Poipu, HI 96756
(808) 742-7661

Sea Sage Diving Center
4-1378 Kuhio Hwy.
Kapaa, HI 96746
(808) 822-3841

Waiohai Beach Service
% Stoffer Waiohai Hotel
Koloa, HI 96756
(808) 742-7051

Wet-N-Wonderful Ocean Sports
P.O. Box 910
Kapaa, HI 96746
(808) 822-0211

Miscellaneous

Plantation Inn
(Bed and Breakfast Inn)
174 Lahainaluna Rd.
Lahaina, HI 96761
(808) 667-9225
(800) 433-6815

APPENDIX 3

USEFUL NUMBER FOR VISITORS

Hawaii Visitors Bureau

The bureau is a privately-funded agency which provides free information on Hawaii. The bureau can help you plan your trip and give you additional information once you reach the islands.

New York
441 Lexington Ave., Room 1407
New York, NY 10017
(212) 986-9023

Washington, D.C.
(Meetings and Conventions)
1511 K Street NW, Suite 415
Washington, D.C. 20005
(202) 393-6752

Chicago
180 N Michigan Ave.
Chicago, IL 60601
(312) 236-0632

Los Angeles
3440 Wilshire Blvd.
Los Angeles, CA 90010
(213) 385-5301

San Fransisco
50 California St.
San Francisco, CA 94111
(415) 392-8173

Japan
630 Shin Kokusai Building, 4-1
3-Chrome, Maruno-uchi, Chiyoda-ku
Tokyo, Japan 100

Hawaii

Oahu
2270 Kalakaua Ave.
Honolulu, HI 96815
(808) 923-1811

Hawaii: The Big Island
180 Kinoole St., Suite 104
Hilo, HI 96720
(808) 961-5797

Kona Plaza Shopping Arcade
Alii Drive
Kailua-Kona, HI 96740
(808) 329-7787

Kauai
3016 Umi St.
Lihue, HI 96766
(808) 245-3971

Weather Forecasts

Island Weather

Kauai	245-6001
Oahu and Honolulu	836-0121
Maui	877-5111
Haleakala	572-7749
Hawaii	961-5582
Hilo	935-8555
Volcanoes National Park	967-7311

Marine Weather

Kauai	245-3564
Oahu and Honolulu	836-3921
Maui	877-3477
Hawaii	935-9883

APPENDIX 4

ADDITIONAL RECOMMENDED DIVE SITES

Listed here are 21 additional recommended sites. When you have tried all the main locations and are ready for something new, be sure to ask your divemaster or dive shop about these spots.

Honolulu County

1. **Black Cave (Big Mouth Cave)** is a boat dive located on the leeward side of Lahilahi Point, in 40 to 90 feet of water. The huge cave offers lots of invertebrates and whitetip reef shark. This site is recommended for intermediate to advanced divers because of depth and occasional strong currents.

2. **Kahe Point (Electric Beach)** is a shore dive on the leeward side of Oahu at Kahe Beach Park. Swarms of tropical fishes are attracted by the electric plant's warm water outflow pipe in 20 to 25 feet of water. This site is recommended for intermediate divers.

3. **Portlock Point** is a 60-foot dive off the southeastern shore of Oahu that offers interesting lava formations and lots of coral and colorful tropicals. This site is recommended for intermediate to advanced divers because of strong currents and surge.

4. **Blow Hole** is a shore dive located off the southeastern shore of Oahu, recommended for advanced divers because of difficult entries and exits as well as occasional strong currents. The interesting terrain offers a good place to find eels and shells in 40-foot depths.

5. **Fantasy Reef** is a 40–60 foot boat dive, where novice and intermediate divers will find lots of tropical reef fish, eels and lobster in an area dominated by ledges and arches.

6. **Kahala Barge**, on the south shore of Oahu, is a 200-foot artificial reef that lies in 50–80 feet of water. This boat dive offers swarms of tropical fish and turtles. This site is recommended for advanced divers because of heavy currents.

Maui County

1. **Monolith** is a boat dive off the southwest corner of Lanai in 40 to 110-foot depths, recommended for advanced divers. The vertical drop-off offers black coral, eels, octopuses and unusual nudibranchs.

2. **Menpachi Cave**, a boat dive off of Lanai, offers a 100-foot long lava tube in 40–60 feet of water and is recommended for intermediate divers. There are a variety of invertebrates and shells are plentiful.

3. **Grand Canyon**, also a boat dive off of southern Lanai, is a submarine canyon in 20 to 100-foot depths that is an ideal place to see turtles and rays. It is reached by boat. This site is recommended for intermediate to advanced divers.

4. **Turtle Haven (Turtle Town)**, a boat dive off northeastern Lanai, offers lush coral gardens in 30-foot depths. This site is recommended for novice divers and is an excellent place to see green turtles.

5. **Tank and Landing Craft** are boat dives off southeastern Maui near Makena, that offer a coral-encrusted WW II tank and landing craft in 60 feet of water. The site is recommended for intermediate divers because currents can be quite strong.